To Carol

From another life I knew....

How now, spirit! whither wander you?
—A Midsummer Night's Dream, Act II, scene i.

I have written the tale of our life
For a sheltered people's mirth,
In jesting guise—but ye are wise,
And you know what the jest is worth.

—Rudyard Kipling

Truly to speak, and with no addition,
We go to gain a little patch of ground
That hath in it no profit but the name.

—A soldier on his way to battle
in *Hamlet*, Act IV, scene iv.

CONTENTS

Foreword 6

Acknowledgements 7

Introduction 8

A Special Hell 12

Blood on the Moon 23

Sleepers, Awake! 31

The Quick and the Dead 37

Fate's Children 44

Notes From the Otherworld 52

The Bridge to Nowhere 56

Death's High Holiday 63

Fields of Sorrows 72

The First Deaths 81

The Last Court of Appeal 87

Endnotes 92

FOREWORD

Mark Nesbitt has gathered a group of ghost tales which seem to support his claim that "Gettysburg may very well be, acre for acre, the most haunted place in America." Certainly the wealth of paranormal experiences he has collected in four books reminds us that either the writer and those he interviewed all have vivid imaginations, or we need to consider the likelihood that what they experienced actually happened. This is not easy, for we live in an age skeptical of things that defy scientific explanation, and reluctant to embrace the mystical feelings and associations we may have when visiting the Battlefield. While we all seem to agree with a definition of Gettysburg as "hallowed ground," we are not comfortable in coming to terms with what that means. As the writer Ed Linenthal points out in *Sacred Ground: Americans and Their Battlefields,* "With the exception of Native American peoples, Americans are not used to classifying their land as sacred. Holy land is elsewhere...."

If our generation is reluctant to talk about things seen and unseen, this was not true of the Civil War veterans, and the rhetoric of their reunion speeches in return visits to Gettysburg was filled with references to the "spirit of place," the "voices" of dead comrades, and the importance of contemplating the meaning of their sacrifices on sacred ground. For example, William J. Ayres, when addressing the veterans of the 95th Pennsylvania Volunteers on July 2, 1888 remarked:

> As we stand here together, as we remember how nobly and bravely life's work was done, let us imagine around about us are the spirits of the brave comrades dead and gone, those who stood with you when you took your solemn oath, and as we leave to them their pure and noble fame, as we leave this spot so sacred, so memorable, may we go forth exalted by this communion, and may we take up life's daily duties and responsibilities manfully.

Of course, perhaps the most eloquent reunion address to evoke the "spirit of place" was given by Maj. Gen. Joshua L. Chamberlain at the dedication of the 20th Maine monument on Little Round Top on October 3, 1889. Often quoted in recent years, it begins: "In great deeds something abides. On great fields something stays. Forms change and pass; bodies disappear; but spirits linger, to consecrate ground for the vision-place of souls." To Mark Nesbitt, those he has interviewed in this book, and Joshua Chamberlain, those spirits unquestionably linger!

Dr. Walter L. Powell
March 13, 1998

ACKNOWLEDGEMENTS:

First I must issue a blanket "Thank You," to the hundreds of people who have written to me explaining their paranormal experiences at Gettysburg. Forgive me for not answering all of you, but it would be literally impossible for me to do so and still research and write books. Your stories are all fascinating, and may just end up in one of the books some day.

But there are some who directly influenced this particular book with their assistance or stories:

Thanks go to Mollie Back, Ghosts of Gettysburg Candlelight Walking Tours™ guide, Robert Bardsley, photographer, and Linda Bell with appreciation for playing "Taps" for the fallen at "The Gettysburg Gate." Thanks to Tim Bowman, one of the young lions, historian Elwood Christ, my good friend Greg Coco, and Jim Cooke and Dave Crockett, spirits of the early morning airwaves. My appreciation to Basil Crapster, Cecil Downing, Doug Dziama, his wife Karlene, and his daughters Susan and Jennifer, Joe Farrell, and longtime friend from when the Visitor meant everything, Paula Fink. Thanks as well go to Rick Fisher from the Pennsylvania Ghost Hunters Society, Jim Garrahy, Marine, Jim and Donna Hoey and the late Michael Hofe (God speed, Mike, and thanks). To Karyol Kirkpatrick, Diana Loski, Peter Monahan, owner of Larson's Motel and Lee's Headquarters Museum—thanks, friends. Fred Moore, Guy Nasuti, Richard Noble, Raye Passmore, and Matt O'Brien all helped with their fabulous stories. Thanks to Dr. Walter Powell, warrior for the good cause, Amie Purdy, Mary Saladna, Pam Saylor, Danette Taylor, Carolyn Thomas, Lori Thorne, Mary Wingert, and Brian Wolle. And special thanks to Sarah Rodgers, my editor at Thomas Publications, and to Dean and Jim Thomas.

INTRODUCTION

The stories keep coming in.

While organizing my material for this fourth book in the *Ghosts of Gettysburg* series, it seemed as if I was never going to get through the stack of letters and notes and photographs sent to me by people who have had some sort of unexplainable experience at Gettysburg. Piled up, the stack was easily a foot high after I went through it a second time. It took me nearly five weeks to read them all, analyze them for content and categorize them into venue. Some of the letters date back to 1994—before *Ghosts of Gettysburg III*, was written.

In addition to the stories there are a number of remarkable things that have come to light because of the books. First, the photos.

Though I have received numerous photos of strange images, I have never included "ghost photographs"—with one or two exceptions— in any of the three other books on ghosts I have written. The reason was because I was never sure how they would reproduce. My concern was threefold: 1) that they should appear in thousands of books, and because of the printing technique, would not show anything "ghostly"; 2) that they would show something not faithful to the original photograph and therefore be misleading to the reader; and 3) because I simply was not convinced that the photos might not just be aberrations in the developing technique, or something the photographers did while snapping the shot, that caused a "ghostly" image to appear.

However, over the last several years, I have received a number of quite remarkable photos, most of which were taken by amateur photographers (it seems like everyone who visits Gettysburg carries a camera) and some of which were taken by professional photographers. Virtually all were taken with no expectation of capturing a "ghost" on film. In fact, the one exception was the professional who took nearly 1,000 photos, many in the notorious "Triangular Field," and was disappointed to announce that not a single one showed anything out of the ordinary. And there was the instance where a local TV crew came in to document the experiences of an earlier crew whose equipment failed. As if to prove its palpable and interactive existence, "something" caused both cameras to fail.

I classify "ghost" photos into two general categories: Those seemingly showing an energy source not visible to the photographer at the time the photo was made; and what I call the "matrix" variety.

The matrix type will usually show a photograph of a group of trees, or rocks, or perhaps an open field of wheat or grass. The photographer and friends will see somewhere in the matrix field a face, or a body outlined by the leaves or shadows on the rocks, or in the windblown grass. And while they may have actually taken a photo of something paranormal, I have to excuse many of the photos because it is like looking at a Van Gogh or at the clouds in a summer's sky: if you use your imagination you can see almost anything you want—sailing ships, faces, the Virgin Mary, Abraham Lincoln, Elvis.

But the other types are most interesting. They show a brightness on the photo, an energy source that illuminates just a section of the picture. Sometimes the source is blue or green; sometimes it is bright white. Sometimes it shows up as a ball of light; sometimes as a streak or blur. Most times the photographer will explain that the image was not visible when they snapped the picture, which means that it was just a momentary emission of energy, occurring coincidentally with and lasting only as long as the shutter was open.

I have talked to professional photographers and developers, and their opinion is that the images could be what are called "lens flares,"—but only if they have sharp edges reflecting the edges of the shutter after it had opened. There is also the possibility that the images came from an over-application of developing emulsion, or something in the darkroom that inadvertently over-exposed the print. Yet some of the photos have come from professionals who did their own developing, sometimes repeating the process several times to make sure everything was done correctly.

Polaroid film seems to be the most sensitive, but it is also prone to showing smears or lights, since the developing technique and film handling are not very controlled, as they would be in a photo lab. As well, there is no opportunity to redevelop the film to see if there might have been something in the mechanical processing to cause the anomaly.

But certain modern developments in cameras—in particular, digital cameras—leave no opportunity for a foul-up in developing. The images come right off the disk to be viewed in the small screen in the back of the camera, with no developing emulsion, no human handling of the film at all.

Recently I had the opportunity to meet some "experts" in ghost photography. They have taken many photos which they consider to be images of spirit phenomena and have classified what they have captured into three general categories: 1) "Globes" of light energy; 2) Fog-like, shapeless or partially-shaped, translucent images which they call "ectoplasm"; and 3) seemingly solid, white "vortexes." They have examined many of the photographs sent to me by others and have confirmed that, indeed, the photographers may have captured the spirits of individuals in places that once contained their earthly bodies. Or, at least they caught the same phenomena in their photos as did the people who were using special techniques and taking photos for the specific purpose of capturing a spirit on film.

The photos have been carefully selected to eliminate those which may be of the matrix variety, and those which may just show some sort of common photographic error in either the making of the picture or the developing. Several are published herein, as well as one photo taken by the author on his first try at "spirit photography."

Another remarkable thing is the volume of unexplainable experiences that apparently have occurred at Gettysburg. People who have never had a paranormal experience in their lives write to me; they come to Gettysburg and there, in a vacant field they see a lone soldier, or perhaps several, moving as if going into battle, or retreating as if they have seen entirely too much of life and death, moving, moving, then...vanishing. People write about hearing strange things: drum taps, bugles, orders being shouted, bagpipes, screams, curses, whisperings. And of smelling out-of-place odors like sulfur smoke, or burning pipe tobacco, or decaying meat. They describe being physically touched, as if someone had grabbed them or tapped them on the shoulder, or as if they had stepped on something that felt uneasily like flesh and bone beneath their foot, and finding nothing when they tried to examine the source. They write of the feelings and the visions they have just being *at* Gettysburg; of some sort of connection with another world that is so close it can be reached in an instant, if everything is just right, if the time is right, and the attitude is right. Whatever it is that they are seeing seems to be sensitive to our feelings as well—more sensitive perhaps of ours than we are of its feelings—and so would seem intelligent in that it reacts to us on at least a psychic level.

Finally, I am amazed that there are people out there who still claim that nothing paranormal is happening at Gettysburg. I am amazed because of the sheer volume of letters I have in my files from people who have had a paranormal experience at Gettysburg. This is the fourth book, but I have enough accounts for another book, and perhaps another after that. The stories of people's experiences, if nothing else, provide a body of data that can be analyzed, like a sociological study, to extract patterns.

There are still many out there who refuse to believe either me, or the seeming phenomena that occur at rare places upon the earth, or the average, normal people who experience these things and, though reluctant, feel compelled for honesty's sake (and in spite of the fact that they risk being humiliated by non-believers) to share their experience. Historians (of which, in Gettysburg, there is a superabundance) and pseudo-historians (of which there are even more) have numerous reasons for denying the obvious fact that large numbers of visitors have had unexplainable—perhaps even paranormal—experiences here. Oddly, many of the historians cannot say why *they* have been drawn to Gettysburg— "A feeling, when I was very young that I was supposed to be here," or something even less logical. Even stranger, is the primary source material for the stories....

For the explanation of the Battle of Gettysburg, we have several "primary" sources: the Official Records, which are reports that were written shortly after the action and often reflect a defensiveness (if the subject unit behaved poorly or was defeated in the battle) or an overstatement of the unit's participation. So, rather than being unimpeachable sources, the O.R.'s are necessarily biased.

Then there are the memoirs of individual soldiers, tainted by the same bias as the O. R.'s, but with the curse of hindsight, necessitating the individual to either overly defend his unit's (or his own) actions. In addition you have the unique phenomenon called "The Fog of War," which is another term for memory failure brought on by the trauma of combat. And, believe it or not, you have some outright lying, which, as any historian will acknowledge, occurred more frequently than any of us would like to admit.

As well, any witnesses to the Battle of Gettysburg are all dead. Getting them into a courtroom to raise their right hands and swear upon a Bible that their account of the battle is exactly the way it happened is problematic. Therefore, questioning them is out of the question.

However, if you would like to question any of the primary sources for the stories in this book, the eyewitnesses (provided they are willing) are available for questioning. Like I always say to my fellow historians: . you put your primary sources on the witness stand and I will put mine on, and we will see who gets the better answer.

Interestingly enough, one of the main complaints scientific types have about "ghost experiences" is that they cannot be replicated in a laboratory. To this there are two answers:

1) The experiences can be classified as "anecdotal;" in other words, they happen very infrequently or perhaps just once. That, of course, is no reason to discount the event and claim that it never happened and that the observer must be mistaken. Many scientists agree on the "Big Bang" theory of creation which apparently happened only once, was witnessed by no one, and cannot be replicated in a laboratory.

2) Some researchers have been able to locate and photograph what they believe are spirit entities at certain places—cemeteries, battlefields—and can predict, by using scientific instruments, where the invisible entities are located for photographing. In other words, they *can* replicate their results time and again, in certain "laboratories."

But the final statement on whether ghosts at Gettysburg exist comes from the National Park Service, a branch of the United States Government. When I was a park ranger at Gettysburg, we were told to say that there are no ghosts at Gettysburg. To my knowledge, they are still reciting the party line. That in itself tells you something. As we have seen countless times before, if the government is denying it, there *must* be something to it!

A SPECIAL HELL

...the members of the 99th, every man of them looked like ghosts, and it was not until after I made the discovery that I came to the conclusion they thought I was the only man in the regiment not frightened half out of his senses....

— Color Sgt. Harvey May Munsell,
99th Pennsylvania Infantry[1]

Devil's Den. The name echoes down through time like a great gong ringing the death knell of a thousand boys in butternut and blue.

It would, at first, seem like a good place to fight. Combat, like some twisted child's game, demands hiding places and cover and surprise. And all this the immense rocks and boulders of Devil's Den provide. But trying to move men through the labyrinth in battle lines was impossible, and so the fight took on the characteristics of what some of the men called Indian fighting: peering around corners, sprinting from one rock to another, never knowing when you will round a corner and run right into the muzzle of a loaded musket, or the pointed end of a triangular bayonet.

And the fight for Devil's Den just gobbled men up. Before the Confederates got to the Den, they first had to cross a strange triangular-shaped field. Much of the savage fighting took place there, with waves of men from Texas and Arkansas and Alabama and Georgia fighting men from New York and Maine and Indiana and Pennsylvania. Hanging over the rock wall at the top of the Triangular Field were four guns of Smith's 4th New York Battery,[2] no doubt loaded with canister, the deadly, giant shotgun shell used against packed infantry that shredded men into fine bits. In support of the guns were the granite men of the 4th Maine, and the 124th New York, whose major, James Cromwell, seemed too brave for his own good. Twice, as the Rebels advanced up the slope of the Triangular Field the 22-year-old requested of his regimental commander, Col. A. Van Horne Ellis that they attack the disorganized Texans who led the assault. The men around him objected when he mounted his horse in the tempest of fire, saying, "The men must see us today." Ellis finally gave permission for Cromwell to charge. Within minutes the major went down with a bullet in his heart. Imploring his men to save their major, Ellis rose in his stirrups and took a soft lead minie ball in the head. The men of the 124th New York, affectionately nicknamed, "The Orange Blossoms," the pride of their home county of Orange,

New York, were within minutes of annihilation when they withdrew from their exposed position in the oddly-shaped farm field. Roughly forty-one per cent of the Orange Countians would never see their homes again, or would see them as changed men, either physically—missing an arm or leg or hand—or mentally, as men who had seen too much horror to ever be the same again.

After the withdrawal of the 124th New York, things happened quickly. Alabamians charged through the Triangular Field and into the jumble of boulders beyond it. Some men advanced boulder to boulder through a place soon to be appropriately named by men who helped it gain its name with others' blood, "The Slaughter Pen." Texans held the crest above, but only for a while.

Again like a child's game of "Capture the Flag," the fighting continued through the maze of rocks. But instead of children's instruments of sticks and tin cans, drawing shouts and peals of laughter, more hideous implements drew screams and shrieks and low, agonized moans of the wounded.

Soon the Texans were driven from the crest by the men from Maine and Pennsylvania. Fighting in and for their home state, they had a greater stake in this battle than any other troops there.

The bodies of Cromwell and Ellis were stretched out on a large boulder to the rear of the remnants of their reformed line. Other officers fell, crumpled on the sparse spots of flat ground; still more bodies were folded awkwardly, painfully wedged between the unforgiving rocks. Down the slope a ways could be seen through the battle smoke a disembodied, bloody hand and arm eerily waving back and forth, back and forth....[3]

Georgians now took over the unwelcome duty of advancing up the slope of the Triangular Field and through the ravine formed by the huge boulders of Devil's Den and the side of Big Round Top along Plum Run. Men were killed in every way imaginable, as if Death itself were some infinitely creative artist painting the Apocalypse. A popular officer was felled when an artillery shell exploded in front of him and a fragment struck him in the head. A soldier passed him "laying on his back with half his head shot off."[4] Another man was shot through the top of his head, victim of the overhead position of the Yankees higher on the rocks.

The Confederates in the Slaughter Pen were attacked by men from the 40th New York Infantry, but it was in vain; the rest of the Union troops in the area were about to begin a retreat. At about the same time, Georgians united with Texans and overran Devil's Den.

The 99th Pennsylvania's Color Guard was particularly obstinate about leaving the ground of their native state. Perhaps it was because of a premonition of death and resignation to it that eighteen-year-old, baby-faced George Broadbent from nearby Lancaster, Pennsylvania fought as he did. Firing until nearly his last cartridge, he turned to his color sergeant to ask what they would do when the ammunition ran out. Turning his head meant the Rebel minie ball smashed into his temple and, according to the color sergeant, "He fell to the earth, the blood squirting out of the bullet hole over his battle begrimed face."

Part of the Slaughter Pen.

Broadbent's friend Charles Herbster came over to the body, took out his handkerchief and wiped the blood off the child's face. In an act only soldiers can understand, he bent and kissed the boy's gentle face, then planted himself on his knees behind the body and, along with another man from Lancaster, began firing as fast as he could. As the regiment got the order to retire, the color sergeant told them they should come along, but they would not leave the Broadbent boy. The next day, the sergeant found Herbster, dead and lying across the body of his young friend who he had refused to leave, even in death. It turned out that Herbster, too, had talked of a premonition of dying a few hours before the battle....

And the color sergeant Munsell—as he retreated with the regiment a shell excavated a hole in front of him. Stunned by the explosion he fell headlong into it. When he awoke he was within Confederate lines and so he "played 'possum," until a surge of Federal troops "recaptured" his shell-hole. Some of the Union troops in the area must have thought him a ghost, or perhaps recalling their scripture, feared that this was the day of judgment as Munsell rose from the very earth like a figure from the Great Resurrection.[5]

George Branard, color bearer of the 1st Texas, mounted the highest rock in Devil's Den, and there planted the Lone Star Flag of Texas. Making a special target of himself, it was not long before a Union artillerist lobbed a shell at him that smashed the flag staff and sent the gallant color bearer tumbling from his perch.

But the Confederates were in Devil's Den to stay. Some perhaps, remain to this very day, men lost in battle, now lost somewhere in time....

There are photos of the dead in twisted positions among the rocks, but the descriptions from Union soldiers who visited the site after the battle, as quoted in Garry Adelman's and Timothy Smith's outstanding book, *Devil's Den: A History and Guide,* are even more horrifying than the photos. Men, in their death agonies, had torn up leaves and grass, and bitten into the good earth with their teeth, ending their lives with their mouths filled with dirt.

Some of the Confederates had been "buried" by tossing them into the cracks and fissures between the rocks of Devil's Den, since the surface soil there is minimal. Some bodies were washed down Plum Run into large piles and there decomposed, their earthly beings co-mingled with the elements. Some of the Confederates were wounded and fell into the crevices, trapped there to die slowly or drown in the torrential rains and rising waters of July 4. Some of the glorious dead were merely dragged together and covered over with brush and a few stones as sepulture. Others were dropped into the clefts and had stones piled upon them. As late as October 1863, the odor of decomposing bodies was so strong as to be nearly "strangling" to visitors.

Do the Dead wonder how things turned out? From wherever they are, do they wonder who won this great battle that ripped them from their own existence? Do they still wonder about the outcome of the great thing that meant as much as their own death to them, and that is why they return to this "deathless field"? Or, as soon as they are killed are they suddenly "translated"? Do they immediately know from their point of view, how things will turn out? Do they suddenly get some great overview of eternity? Or is time linear for them too? Do they have to wait, wherever they are, for the cosmic clock to keep ticking, day in, day out, "tomorrow and tomorrow and tomorrow," piling one upon another to see the outcome of this theater of life, "to the last syllable of recorded time"? It is an interesting question. But fear not. We all will know the answer to it, sooner or later....

Like the tiny, unseen molecules emanating from the last essences of what were once dear brothers and husbands and sons to assault the visitors' olfactory nerves, there are other usually unseen entities that assault the senses of modern visitors to this place named after the dwelling place of the Devil.

Devil's Den had legends circulating about it even before the battle. The area, without government roads, was truly a maze for local hunters in the early days. There is the story that comes down to us from hunters who got lost in the area and saw a quiet stranger beckoning them to follow him. He stayed just far enough ahead so that they could not talk to him or tell who he was. He motioned for them to follow and, trusting, they did, until they eventually found their way out of the rocky tangle. When they looked for him to thank him, he had vanished.[6]

The battlefield has been a Mecca for curious visitors almost since the fighting ended. First there were those who came right after hearing about the great man-consuming battle to try to find loved ones who had been with the army. Later, after hearing that loved ones had died, they came to claim the bodies, sometimes having to endure the agony of watching their dear one's countenance—or what was left of it—slowly emerge from a hastily scratched grave. Perhaps the most poignant were the veterans who returned with a sweetheart or wife a few months or a couple of years later to walk the fields where they once came so close to the Grim Reaper that they could smell his fetid breath.

A woman and her husband were visiting Gettysburg in September 1996 as a means of relaxation from their grueling jobs. She admitted that prior to that visit, the Civil War was pretty much meaningless to her and her husband. In her words, "Devil's Den could have been Bedrock...Longstreet, Pickett could have been the names of streets in Gettysburg as far as we knew. I'm embarrassed to say that." She need not be embarrassed anymore. That night she and her husband were given a history lesson that they will never forget, a lesson seemingly taught by the original participants.

It was close to 10:00 p.m., closing time for the park. They decided that they would risk getting caught and stay a little longer in Devil's Den, figuring that with everyone else out of the park, it would be nice and quiet. They were soon to discover that just because the park is closed, it does not mean that things are quiet.

She readily admitted that she and her husband were staying, "in hopes of seeing or hearing something out of the ordinary." They ran into another woman and a married couple who lived near Gettysburg. Together they walked along the winding road through Devil's Den and reached the spot where it begins to curve upward into the jumble of boulders. From behind them in the dark distance but approaching rapidly, they heard the sound of galloping hooves. Who in the world, they thought, would be riding at such a breakneck pace through the dark and in such a dangerous place? Only someone on a life and death mission would risk that speed among the jumble of rocks. They heard the rhythmic clopping pound louder and louder as the horse (apparently with a rider) approached. They also heard the horse snorting and panting through its nostrils. The little group of five hustled to get off the road and out of the way of the galloper before he ran over them in his urgency. As they scrambled to move out of the way, just as suddenly as it had been heard, the sound of the horseman was gone. No horse or rider ever appeared, although, at least according to the racket he was making, he was nearly upon them.

"The men must see us today!"

They stood in the darkness, wondering at what had just occurred. To calm themselves they all sat on one of the large rocks and began to share some coffee from a thermos. Their resting place was about fifty feet from the road where they had just encountered the phantom horseman. As the woman recalled, the moonlight was perfect and it was a beautiful warm fall night. Attempting to brush aside their somewhat unnerving experience, they

16

began to exchange pleasantries about families, jobs, the weather. They joked and laughed—somewhat nervously—for a few minutes. Then the single woman said that she needed to stretch her legs and got up to take a walk. She had no sooner left the rock, when the two couples heard something strange and unmistakable coming from the road.

Cleats. On the hard road. And voices. The muffled voices of men. Slowly, hazily out of the fabulous darkness could be seen emerging the forms of five individuals, walking slowly, painfully, near where the modern road bends, heading toward the Triangular Field. They were not, however, following the modern road. As if they were ignorant of a road, or perhaps as if the road did not exist for them, they crossed along the route of least resistance, across and between the great, immovable rocks of Devil's Den. The woman described them as follows: "Yes, they were Union soldiers, the shape of their kepis, the collars, all of their uniforms. You could see their guns...." Some carried weapons on their shoulders, some at their sides. They walked, as the woman related, "in a slow motion, defeated, worn out fashion." The modern visitors stood transfixed by the slow passage of soldiers from out of time. Then suddenly, as if plucked back into the era from where they had been given a temporary leave of absence, they vanished, back apparently into an hour and day when the Devil did hold high court in his own den.

The woman said that from the route the men were taking she was "waiting to hear screaming because they were about to get seriously hurt or even killed if they fell from the huge rocks." But as the poet Dylan Thomas observed, *After the first death, there is no other....*

The woman who had gone to stretch her legs suddenly came running back, shouting, "You won't believe what I just saw!" She repeated it, but the two couples were speechless. As the woman put it, she—and apparently the others—had trouble expressing what they had just seen, since it appeared to be completely illogical. Finally, someone in the group answered the woman. During the ensuing discussion, it slowly came to light that they had all seen the same thing: the number of men, their uniforms, their weapons, their attitude, their route across the rocks, and their mysterious disappearance.

She then related something that they, and many others who have had an encounter with inhabitants of the Other World, have felt in common: "The greatest fear of all was the bone-chilling cold that befell on all of us. Mind now, it was Sept. 14th, [but] it felt like we had walked into a walk-in freezer. The chill started at your ankles and overwhelmed your whole body. To speak a word would take an act of God, because you can't utter a sound as they were passing in front of us. Hoping and praying that no one would holler or even breathe, that you would attract their attention...."

She concluded by writing: "We all departed mutually agreeing what we all had just seen. I know what I saw and if you ever have the good fortune to experience an event like this, you will never forget it. You automatically want to learn more about that time period and really what happened there.... Let me tell you, I now read, view any literature I can find to educate us on the Civil War, Gettysburg and also all the Generals involved at that time."

"As God is my witness I know what I saw."

The best teachers teach more than facts and figures, dates and names. They interest us enough in a subject so that we will go on learning long after class is out.

Good teachers they were indeed to come all the way from another century to impress upon their unsuspecting students, a lesson in immortality....

A group of college students were visiting Gettysburg around the time of the anniversary of the battle in 1993. Some of their friends who lived in the area thought it might be fun to take them to Devil's Den. Jokingly they told them to expect to see ghosts. Having purchased *Ghosts of Gettysburg* and *More Ghosts of Gettysburg*, they had read them just a few hours before. And so they laughed half nervously at their friends' prediction. Unfortunately, someone had thought to bring along a Ouija Board.[7]

It was after dark. One young man was exploring the labyrinth of boulders where, one hundred and thirty years before, nearly to the day, close to eight thousand men about his age had risked or given up their lives and futures for a few yards of rock-strewn Pennsylvania real estate. When he returned to his group, they excitedly claimed that they had "contacted" a dead Union soldier through the Ouija Board.

His name, as it was spelled out on the Ouija Board, was "Airck," which they quickly translated to "Eric." He was not alone. They asked who accompanied him in whatever world he was occupying. Haltingly, the board spelled out "Q...D." First and last initials perhaps—the Ouija is never forthright—but someone in the group thought it could be a fond nickname given by the soldier to his loved one. They called her "Cutie."

They proceeded to ask him many questions, for which they received a few answers, many cryptic, some enlightening, many more playful. *They are such pranksters, those of the spirit world....*

It was getting close to 10:00 p.m., and they knew the park closed at that time. They decided to say goodbye to the "spirits" they had contacted. Just before they signed off, one of the young men asked a quick question: Would Airck and QD meet them at their cars in the parking lot across from Devil's Den?

One of the men, who had had several bad experiences with Ouija Boards and spirits, became immediately frightened. They packed up the board and began to descend the carved rock steps toward the parking lot. The young man who had flippantly asked the spirit to meet them at their cars was leading along with one of the young women. Another young man wrote that he could feel the tension in the air. As he and another young woman followed the first couple, suddenly he heard the young lady shriek. From the darkened parking lot the young man who had summoned the spirits through the mystical board cried, "Oh, My God!"

The rest of the group ran down the rock stairs. The collegian at the bottom was already pointing into the woods across from the parking lot—across the infamous Slaughter Pen—with his mouth frozen open, repeating, over and over, "Do you see them? Do you see them?" Another couple in the parking lot simultaneously leapt back from the woods and yelled that they did.

There, slowly emerging from the woods and approaching Plum Run where it sloughs through the Slaughter Pen, was a man—or at least what they thought was a human—dressed in blue. He appeared to be wearing old-time trousers, what anyone who has seen the old photographs would call Union Army issue. Upon his head he wore a cap. The strangest thing about the man was that he had no face, no features. Emanating from his "body" was a bluish-gray tinge. As he strolled slowly, the young people could discern yet another figure—that of a woman—slowly keeping pace alongside her soldier. Indeed she was with him, in both space and time, since she was quite fashionable in her mid-nineteenth century gown.

The eerie couple walked directly toward the two cars the young people had driven to Devil's Den. Suddenly it seemed like a foot race to see who could reach the cars first. The young man who had called forth the spirits and the others quickly piled into both cars. As they sped away into the darkened labyrinth of tumble-down boulders which once felt the sting of hot lead and the sticky damp of mens' lifeblood trickling down them, one brave

The parking lot at Devil's Den and the bridge across Plum Run.

young man had the courage to look back. There, from the woods, he saw frozen, as if disappointed that their rendezvous had been abruptly canceled, a blue radiance, fading slowly into nothingness.

Anyone who has driven Devil's Den at night knows that the twisting, curling road seems to go nowhere, and a wrong turn can bring you right back to where you do not want to be. There are two upward climbing, hairpin turns: one goes right by the stone barricade where the poor soldier of the South was dragged for a photographer's whimsy. Up a little farther is Smith's Battery, the once deadly muzzles of its guns which sent scores of men to their Maker—or to His most horrible Counterfeit if they had not lived good lives—and which must be passed to continue the ride through Devil's Den. Just when you think you are about to emerge from the jumble of rocks, you realize that to your left is the Triangular Field, home or eternal prison to a number of souls who dislike photographers with an unearthly passion. Then you are plunged into the woods again, a dark tunnel which must be traversed. When you emerge from the tunnel, you are now in the Wheatfield, where, for a few hours on July 2, 1863, men were the fruitful and overabundant harvest, later to become the richest fertilizer ever strewn upon that—or any other—field of wheat.

And just when you think you have passed out of the frightful places, you are once again immersed in dark woods. Your car lights swing to the left and you see before you another hairpin turn and...what is that before you? A man. No, the back of a man, turned away, entirely bleached, white as bones left in the sun too long. It must be just a statue, but he appeared so abruptly, and as the car headlights strike him...look, look, his head! Is he turning to look at us?

The group of college students admitted to a great deal of trouble sleeping the next two nights. They did return the next day, however, to investigate the area of their most unusual sighting. They found a few footprints—not unusual for a tourist Mecca—a bike track, and a straight, thin line, made by an old fashioned umbrella or stick, but nothing out of the ordinary. They left Devil's Den and Gettysburg with a newly found respect for that old phrase, *Don't wish too hard for what you want...for you just might get it.*

Apparently, they were not finished tweaking the tail of whatever it is that lives within the mysterious Ouija Board. One final paragraph from the letter they sent me:

Also, we contacted QD the next day and asked her if we had seen them. She said yes. She told us she was waving and that Brian should not have looked so scared.

He said he really wished he knew if anyone else has contacted a QD or an Airck. Which leads us to a letter I received two and a half years later.

A woman wrote and told of several experiences she had during her visit to the area below Little Round Top near Devil's Den. She wrote that she is a firm believer in ghosts and has had several paranormal experiences herself. But she never expected what was awaiting her in the part of Devil's Den that earned the gruesome name of the Slaughter Pen.

She recalled visiting, with a friend, a section of the battlefield just below Little Round Top. They were both dressed in replica Civil War clothing, once again producing the appearance of the battlefield in a more ominous time period. (Recall that a survey of the more than two hundred stories collected for the *Ghosts of Gettysburg* series shows a pattern: That whenever the physical status quo of a historical site is altered—and especially when it is being restored to its original appearance—it seems as if there is more likelihood for a paranormal event.)[8]

They were walking around Little Round Top. Her friend was walking in front of her, showing her some of the more obscure sites when suddenly something tapped her on the shoulder. She turned to see where the touch came from and was shocked to see no one. The hairs on the back of her neck rose and a shiver coursed coldly down her spine. She called to her friend who stopped, turned, and of course, saw nothing either. She suddenly did not want to be the last one in line and so began to walk alongside her friend. As they moved down the hill, she recalled, they passed through several areas where they "could both smell the odor of rotten eggs." Black powder, the main propellant for projectiles in the Civil War, is composed of charcoal, saltpeter and sulfur. The sulfur gives the powder when it burns the distinct aroma of rotten eggs. She also related that her friend, who was dressed in a Confederate medical officer's uniform, "Sometimes...felt a lot of hostility towards himself. Maybe," she speculated, "the ghosts were jealous or maybe they were the souls of departed Yankees, who knows?"

On another occasion, she was visiting the battlefield with a different friend and they took the auto tour. At 9:45 p.m., they stopped to use the restrooms at Devil's Den, which are located across a small, wooden bridge over Plum Run in the area of the Slaughter Pen. They had to park in the same parking area where the collegian with the Ouija Board summoned "Airck," and "QD." Here is her account: "We crossed over a foot bridge on Plum Run. Suddenly out of the corner of my eye, I saw a Southern soldier. As the Park was closing, I was pretty sure the soldier wasn't a reenactor. It seemed to glow a brilliant blue. Needless to say we got the heck out of there!"

Glowing, phosphorescent spectres emerging from the deep woods near a place named appropriately, the Slaughter Pen. The smell of black powder out of time and space where it should have been blown to the far winds thirteen decades past. A lone horse galloping where thousands of men once fought, and cleated footsteps wearily making their way back from a battle that ended in the mid-nineteenth century. A tapping on the shoulder at a venue where much firmer touches once occurred: where the soft lead minie balls traveling at 900 feet per second did their tapping...tapping...tapping in a more permanent fashion two thousand times over at the place called Devil's Den.

Example of spirit photography—"ectoplasm"—at Devil's Den parking lot.
Photo by Rick Fisher, PA Ghost Hunters Society

BLOOD ON THE MOON

This royal throne of kings, this scepter'd isle,
This earth of majesty, this seat of Mars,
This other Eden, demi-paradise,
This fortress built by nature for herself...
This happy breed of men, this little world,
This precious stone set in the silver sea....
                                        —Richard II, Act II, scene i.

It is a mysterious place, this that has been named—at least in this time—Gettysburg. For you see, all that is here on this earth now was once something else, and was used for other things, and perhaps called by other names.

There are so many among us who doubt, who deny their own senses and sensibility about this world, or about this illusion we call reality. Religion perhaps comes closest to explaining it, but if you do not believe in a Heaven, then religion does not help you much. Theoretical physics comes closest next to explaining existence beyond life: that there could be, alongside of this world, a parallel one, invisible most of the time. And theoretical physics can be proved by perhaps the one immutable in this world: mathematics. And mathematics, as with some things in religion, was ordained before the world began. Two plus two was four before there was a world and anyone in it to know it....

I will be the first to admit that after a quarter of a century living in Gettysburg I have had only four—perhaps five—unexplainable experiences. Some people only have one in their entire life, and so I suppose I must consider myself lucky. Or unlucky.

I am a skeptic, by nature and by training. One of the things you learn early in writing is that you must be a consummate observer; getting involved with your subject as a writer is like prey getting involved with its predator. I try to approach all the subjects I write about objectively. Although it may not seem like it when I write about them, that is the ultimate trick in writing: to convince the reader that I am involved while still being able to interpret dispassionately for them.

There was one experience that I had recently where my curious objectivity could have gotten me into trouble, could possibly have landed me "on the other shore." I was finally so close to my subjects that I literally could have reached out and touched them...or taken a step into their unknown world....

On the evening of January 10, 1998, I met with Rick Fisher, his wife Randee, and his friend Tom Hartman of the Pennsylvania Ghost Hunters Society, per our conversation of a week before when he called me and asked if I wanted to accompany them in attempting to photograph "ghosts" out on the Gettysburg battlefield. We were met in the parking lot of the Jennie Wade House by author Jeff Frazier and his wife Helen.

Of course my skepticism kicked in right away. Scores of people have sent me what they believe are spirit images caught on film. I have been reluctant to publish them for a number of reasons.

In a previous conversation, Rick explained to me his technique for finding and photographing spirits at various historic and tragic sites. Finally, here was a logical (if that term can be applied to the paranormal world) proactive method of going to where spirits may linger, locating their invisible (at least to the human eye) presences, and documenting them in a photograph. At least his method made more sense to me than a medium conjuring up spirits at a card table.

We went into the lobby of the Holiday Inn where Rick showed me some of the recent photos of "ghosts" he had taken at Gettysburg. I was immediately amazed at the similarity between the results of his organized attempts at photographing spirits and the photos I have received over the years from people who have visited Gettysburg, taken pictures and found something strange in a photo that was not there when the shutter was opened.

In many of the photos he identified the three characteristic types of anomalies that he considered evidence of an unidentified source of energy: first, a ball or globe of light, looking very much like a water spot on the print, but visible as well on the negative; second, a misty haze that Rick called "ectoplasm" through which details of the image behind could be seen; and finally, a seemingly solid, apparently whirling streak that he called a "vortex." All three types were visible in the photos that people were kind enough to send me. As well, there was a more personal connection.

As teenagers, my cousin and I had visited Gettysburg innumerable times. We were intensely interested in the battle and the field upon which the great, horrible game, with men's fate as wager, was played out. He went on to become a successful businessman, but never lost his interest in Gettysburg. Or perhaps I should say, the place never released its hold upon him. He is an excellent photographer. Some of his work is truly artistic; he knows composition and has the patience to produce fine work. His daughter is a college student and lives in a sorority house that has the distinction of having been a station on the Underground Railroad. She heard the rumor that there had been a tunnel in the cellar which had been used to spirit runaway slaves clandestinely from the house to another site. Curious, she thought she had seen some evidence of disturbed

24

earth in the cellar and decided to do a little archaeology herself. She showed her father the minor excavation she had been working on and he decided to document it with his camera. When he had the film developed he realized that he had gotten a little more than he bargained for.

Indeed, directly over the excavation was a haze, in some places opaque, in others transparent. To the left of the picture, staring directly at the camera with veiled, hooded eyes was a face; to the right, a profile.

I showed Rick some of the photos that had been sent to me over the years including my cousin's. Rick did not hesitate at the photo. He said it showed the presence of ectoplasm. He also examined the other photos that had been sent to me over the last couple of years. Amazed at some of them, he agreed that they did show what he has identified as the three types of spirit evidence.

I was almost reluctant to leave the comfort of the Holiday Inn lobby. Perhaps I was even stalling a little, because, although I have documented hundreds of others' paranormal experiences, and even have had a few of my own, I never went *looking* for the supernatural. Rick had already done some photography at Devil's Den, the Triangular Field and the Angle with successful results using his special technique. I suggested we go over to the Confederate side of the field and see if he could locate and photograph anything there.

As we turned onto West Confederate Avenue, the battlefield seemed darker than usual, even though it was only 6:00 p.m. The area we were passing through was one of particularly tragic historic import. On July 3, 1863, at about 1:00 p.m., long lines of Confederate infantry hunkered down in the woods to our right while their massed artillery pieces exploded in what was to become one of the largest cannonades on the North American continent. Near where we now rode passed tons of artillery shells from the Union artillery's reply. In the space through which Rick drove, men were literally torn apart by flying artillery shells or liquefied by exploding rounds. Some Confederates were even killed by huge branches being blown off the trees and falling to crush the soldiers below. Not every casualty in war is some noble boy, falling gracefully to the ground, wrapped in his country's flag, as the movies would have us believe. Death visits as a grotesque and savage butcher, sometimes hacking, sometimes bludgeoning his way through his innocent hosts. The area we were driving through was where men prepared themselves to die, just prior to that massive and infamous holocaust of human souls known to history as Pickett's Charge.

We stopped at the Virginia Memorial. While at the Holiday Inn I had shown them two photos that people had sent to me of strange gold spots taken there. One shot was of a reenactment artillery piece with two reenactors standing nearby. There was one of the translucent globes Rick described as entity energy floating just to the right of the caisson. But that was not the thing that interested me. The strangest thing about the photo was what appeared in the background, between the two reenactors, seemingly positioned against the dark of what is known historically as the Point of Woods. There, against the dark woods where men trembled and prayed to the God some were about to meet in mere moments, was a golden cross and what appears to be several gold stars hovering above and to the right of the cross.[1]

For so blatant a religious symbol to appear in a photo of the Gettysburg Battlefield is odd enough. But in November 1996 I received another photo, this one taken from nearly the same spot except that the camera was pointed about 90 degrees to the west of the first photo. It was a typical photo of the Virginia Memorial, with Confederate General Robert E. Lee astride Traveller at the top, and his rag-tag and devoutly loyal men on the base below. What was different about the photo was that just above—or superimposed upon—the head of one of the figures were four or five star-like points of light and a slight haze that spread across the statue's face. In his letter, the photographer wrote that he thought the haze looked like a face and head with a halo. The color of the haze and points of light was golden.[2]

This was the reason I chose the Virginia Memorial and the Point of Woods to visit that night. But as we exited the vehicle and began to gather equipment for our walk out into the darkened killing fields where so many souls had begun their fabulous post-life journey, I began to regret my choice of venues. This indeed was one of the prime killing grounds of the entire world—and of all history—and we were about to invade what must have been—and perhaps still is—a very special place to many now long gone.

We all know the spot where we came into this world: the hospital, the house, or at least the town; it has been recorded legally, for any biographer to see; it has a special hold on us, because it is a special place, where we dropped onto this earth from wherever we were before. But the place of our death is unknown; we cannot—or at least we think we cannot—look and say, "There is where I died," like we can about where we were born. But if we could, then the place where we died must be at least as heart-holding as where we were born—and maybe even more so.

As we stood near the car in the dim light of the open trunk, I asked Rick if there was any mental preparation we needed to do. I know that psychics usually need a certain state of mind to become receptive to the supernatural.

"I usually just talk to them, mentally. I say in my mind, 'It's all right. We're not here to disturb you. We respect and honor you for what you did here. We just want to recognize you. We understand your sacrifice. We hope you are at peace.'" It certainly made sense to me, and, although I repeated similar thoughts during our visit, as strange as it may seem, I myself have spoken to the long-gone men of that war many times before. While working on my book on Joshua Chamberlain, I had an opportunity to visit his grave. I do not remember articulating it, but I suppose I was asking for the general's help in understanding him and his motives and the mysteries of his life. After the book was published, I had an opportunity to visit his grave again; it was a whole different feeling I got standing there the second time. Somehow I felt as if I had gotten the general's approval for my work.

We walked out along the damp macadam that runs alongside the Point of Woods. I had my head down, ostensibly to watch for trip-ups and to warn those behind me of them. But really, I did not want to look into those woods where I had seen the photo of the golden cross. We neared the cluster of benches where the audio station was located, then walked to the south of where the cannons are set up in battery, mute now, but guarding the hallowed site for all eternity. We were walking in the footsteps of the men of Pickett's Division, and parts of two others, those noble and gallant soldiers who launched themselves, 12,000 strong, at the Union line, only to return at one-third their strength, 8,000 of their comrades and brothers and cousins left as human chaff after some mad reaper worked the field gathering in sheaves of souls rather than wheat.

I was given an electromagnetic field meter that indicates when there is a spike in electromagnetic fields. According to Rick, if you walk directly into a spirit energy, the electromagnetic field detector will spike and the small LED light will turn from green to yellow.

Rick's technique for locating spirit energies is rather simple, but stems from the testimony of hundreds of people who have experienced paranormal phenomena. Rick carried a thermal scanner. Paranormal research indicates that preceding encounters with the supernatural, quite often there is a drop in temperature felt by the usually unwilling participants in the encounter. Dr. Charles Emmons, author of *Chinese Ghosts and ESP*, points out that the cold feeling people get comes *before* the sighting, meaning that it is actually a physical cold, rather than the cold one might feel after a frightening event, caused by lowering blood pressure or decreased circulation to smaller capillaries. In other words, there really is a "cold spot" associated with the sighting. This then was Rick's technique. He said that they had had very good luck taking photos in the direction of where the thermal scanner indicated an extreme drop in temperature.

Sure enough, soon after we got there, the scanner began to indicate that there were spots where the temperature was as low as minus 3 degrees, whereas the ambient temperature in the area seemed to be from 30 to 33 degrees. We were to take photos at the site where he was pointing the meter. My camera was having a few problems with the automatic focus and I could not remember how to turn it off, so I had to auto-focus on my hand, then move my hand and snap the picture.

Rick began moving the scanner in a line parallel with the ground. I was standing behind him watching the LED screen on the handle of the instrument. Suddenly the numeric readout began to drop. It went so fast that it skipped fifteen numbers and stopped momentarily at 16 degrees. It continued to drop until it hit minus three degrees—just one degree from its lowest limit. Rick pointed this out to me as a possible location of a spirit being. I took a photo.

Two or three more times he found a low spike in the meter, and we all took photos into the darkness, seemingly at nothing. I noticed that once

Rick found a cold spot he would seem to track it with the thermometer. "Are they moving?" I asked incredulously. "Yes," he said. "They move." My stomach fluttered.

"In response to us?" I asked.

"Yes," he said. "Sometimes they'll gather around as if they are curious or checking us out."

I had in my hand the electro-magnetic detection meter that Rick had given me. I remembered that he had said that often, "ghosts" or "spirit energies," in addition to registering as a cold spot on the thermometer, will often show up as a spike on the electromagnetic field detection meter. But only if you run right into the energy. As Rick turned in a circle the thermometer's scope passed through the Point of Woods, where he got no reading except the ambient temperature. I was transfixed by the LED readout which fluxed from 30 degrees to thirty-three, to thirty-one.

"Tell me the next time you locate a spirit energy," I heard myself saying. "I want to go over to it."

What was I *saying?*

"There," Rick said as he pointed the meter to the south. "There."

"Help me out," I said as I started walking toward where he pointed the meter. I had the electromagnetic detector in my hand. I was unsure of what to expect, or what was going to happen. I just kept walking.

"It's moving," called Rick. "Go a little to your right."

I followed his instructions.

"Now to the left. Wait. There seems to be another one just to the left of you."

Apparently I was attracting them.

I was about a hundred or so feet from the group, far enough away to feel uncomfortably alone in the dark. But, according to Rick, I was not alone.

"Yes," I heard him say. It sounded as if he were smiling. "They seem to be gathering around you."

Suddenly in my mind was the incredible scene I had written about in *Ghosts of Gettysburg*, about my two friends—administrators at Gettysburg College— who had descended the elevator in Pennsylvania Hall and, as the doors opened, involuntarily witnessed a Civil War hospital before them, the same grotesque theater that had occurred on that very spot twelve decades past. All, everyone, including the participants, have wondered what would have happened if they would have stepped off the elevator *into* that other reality. Would they have been held captive, like the orderlies and doctors apparently had been, to toil in that hell forever? And what of me, now walking toward these entities, and they moving toward me? Had I paid enough homage in my talks and writings to the noble, brave souls I was apparently about to meet? Or were they upset with this intrusive writer of their lives and deaths and afterlives? Had I gone too far? Exactly where was that unseen threshold that I must not cross? Upon crossing it could I ever come back to this world? I stopped walking.

My electromagnetic field meter was still not registering anything unusual. Yet Rick was calling across the field to me that he was detecting several cold spots gathering around me. As I moved the meter from side to side, I was vaguely aware of the group taking photos of me and whatever it was I was attracting.

I stood for a couple of minutes in that once horrible field, apparently drawing to me what some people believe are the curious remnants of the men who once suffered, endured, bled and died there. I can never explain how much reverence I have always had for these men who fought at Gettysburg—those who know me understand. And I have found nothing more poignant in all my studies than the possibility that their spirits may, in some cases, have remained near the spot of earth they died for. Suddenly, I almost felt comfortable as they seemed to be gathering in the dark—as if I was finally meeting some old friends—no, heroes of mine—I had written about but was unable, because of their deaths, to meet. Now, here they were....

But there was only one problem: suddenly I began to feel the intense cold that had been slowly surrounding me. By then, the rest of the group had wandered over to where I was standing, and we stood and discussed some of the anomalies we were trying to photograph.

Rick said that when he takes his scanner out in his own back yard, he never gets a low spike in temperature. However, when he takes it to a graveyard or a structure purported to be haunted, or a battlefield, he always runs into extremely negative temperature spots, like the ones we were experiencing tonight.

Finally, I spoke up: "Is anybody else cold? My hands are freezing." I walked away from the group and immediately felt the ambient temperature rise. Relatively speaking, it felt like a heatwave compared to the area where we had just stood.

We walked back and forth in front of the Point of Woods, Rick's spot thermometer dipping from 32 degrees down to minus three again and again. He let me hold the thermometer. I located two or three spots where the temperature plummeted, and I followed them as they moved until I lost them. Where they went, I do not know. They may have risen, since I do not remember pointing the thermometer upward. Cold air does not rise, so it never occurred to me to seek upward. But, apparently we were not dealing with just cold air....

Finally we left. Rick and the rest of the crew wanted to go to Iverson's Pits and see if they could detect anything there. We took a few photos of the Virginia Memorial, where the golden spots had been photographed. Upon returning to the Jennie Wade House, I gave Rick directions to Iverson's Pits and we said goodbye.

It was over a week before I got the film developed. As I sat in the parking lot of the photo shop I casually thumbed through the photos. They were mostly dark, except where the flash reflected off the grass. I saw the Virginia Memorial, two out-of-focus shots of the woods, Rick's hand and arm holding the spot thermometer, the trail of one of the cannons, and four pictures of the darkness and light grass in the foreground. I went through the photos again, looking a little more closely. I smiled to myself as I noticed what appeared to be one of the globes of light I had seen before in the lower left corner of one of the shots. I shuffled a couple more photos, and then I saw it. There, in the center of the photo, just beyond the grass illuminated by the flash, was a bluish gray, upright form.

One must be very careful when confronted with something beyond one's scope of carefully circumscribed reality. There was nothing there when I took the photo; I thought I was just taking pictures of the dark. And with just a little imagination, the figure indeed has something of a human form, considering that when humans are in motion, their bodies turn and twist, their heads bob and duck. The distance away from the camera cannot be determined, so I cannot tell if it is just a torso with no legs close to the edge of the lighted area, or if it is a full figure ten or fifteen feet outside of the light. Upon reflection, however, it reminded me of the unexplainable and mysterious entity I saw behind my house one night several years ago. That is what it looked like. That I can share with you now.

Did I actually catch a photo of a spirit? Has Rick Fisher discovered a way to pinpoint where these entities are so that we can photograph them? And will we ever be able to get a photo that is clear enough to determine facial features or clothing so as to identify the human to whom the spirit once belonged? And, if we did, would any one of us recognize the poor soul as one of our relatives?

Photo taken at the Point of Woods, field of Pickett's Charge.
Ambient temperature: 30-33 degrees. Spot temperature: minus 3 degrees.

SLEEPERS, AWAKE!

...I must watch you from the Spirit-land and hover near you...till we meet to part no more. But, O Sarah! if the dead can come back to this earth and flit unseen around those they loved, I shall always be near you; in the gladest days and in the darkest nights...always, always, and if there be a soft breeze upon your cheek, it shall be my breath, as the cool air fans your throbbing temple, it shall be my spirit passing by. Sarah do not mourn me dead; think I am gone and wait for thee, for we shall meet again....

            — Major Sullivan Ballou, 2nd Rhode Island Volunteers, killed at the Battle of 1st Bull Run one week later.

Dante, the fourteenth century expert on Heaven and Hades, in his wildest dreams, could not have imagined a hell more excruciating than a Civil War hospital. He came close to describing one a couple of times when he wrote: "There is no greater sorrow than to recall a happy time in the midst of wretchedness,"—which, no doubt, most young soldiers try to recall when dangerously wounded. There are accounts of them dictating letters to nurses, many of which talk about a better time in their past, when they were home with their beloved families, safe and sound and free of pain. There are other, more pitiful accounts of grown men, when wounded, crying for their mothers....

As well, Dante summed up rather succinctly a description that would fit both a field hospital and the Lower Regions:

Their sighs, lamentations and loud wailings resounded through the starless air, so that at first it made me weep; strange tongues, horrible language, words of pain, tones of anger, voices loud and hoarse, and with these the sound of hands, made a tumult which is whirling through that air forever dark....

But perhaps he described both hospital and Hades best in his most famous quote, posted above the entrance to Hell: *Abandon hope, all ye who enter here.*

There are a number of areas in and around Gettysburg known as "Hospital Woods." Perhaps the best known is the area where Camp Letterman—site of the largest temporary field hospital of the war—was once located, about a mile east of Gettysburg on the road to York, Pennsylvania.

Other areas, especially along Hospital Road south of Gettysburg between the Baltimore Pike and the Taneytown Road, were established as field hospital sites. And the backroads and byways inside a radius of a dozen or so miles from the center square of Gettysburg are dotted with small blue signs indicating the former presence of doctors, orderlies and kindly volunteer nurses. Farmhouses marked by signs were, of course, sites occupied as well by the horribly maimed and mutilated bodies of once brave soldier-boys, reduced to crying, pleading, bloodless shells of their former selves.

The woods that once sheltered some of the wounded from the state of Mississippi after the first day's fighting are still in existence. Or should we say that descendants of the trees that once provided shade for the Rebels from the deep South are the only things that remain of the area filled with the detritus of brotherly conflict.

But detritus is such a cold noun to use for men who once had bodies and souls, who had fathers and mothers, wives, children and sweethearts left at home to wonder of their fate. So let us give at least two of the faceless sufferers names. From the official records of the brigade we know of Lt. Col. Moseley and of one Maj. Feeney of the 42nd Mississippi, wounded severely and probably taken to those hideous woods. Coldly the record continues: "A large number of the company officers were killed or wounded...."[1]

Near the site were buried many of the men upon whom the surgeons' ministrations were in vain. Gregory Coco in his book, *Wasted Valor: The Confederate Dead at Gettysburg*, indicates that there were about 63 men buried in the area.[2]

But then again, perhaps the descendants of trees that once sheltered the helpless are not the only things remaining of the hospital site once rife with the tortured souls of youth gone cold and lifeless in the service of a misbegotten dream....

As Gettysburg grew, the area to the south and west of where the field hospital for the Mississippians was located became populated with many fine homes. Fortunately, the historic woods was not touched by the development. But it seems that some of the fine, modern homes were touched...by a more mysterious development.

A number of years ago, an elderly woman who wishes to remain anonymous, began to pursue a lifelong dream of traveling after her husband died. Her travels had kept her on the road, away from her lovely, well-kept home sometimes for weeks at a time.

The woman is as solid and stable as anyone. She had never had any paranormal experiences in her entire life. The closest she had ever come to a paranormal experience was when her husband passed away. She told me of the beautiful white cat that she and her husband had owned. When her husband died, and she returned home from the hospital after his death, the cat seemed to know that its master would not be coming home again. The cat died sometime after that.

That was her only "paranormal" experience until she began to spend time away from what she and her husband had considered their dream home. As if to protest her absence, strange occurrences began, and continue up to this writing....

She is a meticulous housekeeper, the kind who has a proper place for every pillow, and a closet-hook for every broom and dust mop. And, of course, while she was gone from the house, she left it immaculate and had a maid visit every two weeks to dust.

She stayed at a friend's house while on the road. One night she was awakened by an uneasiness and sat up in bed to see the full form of her friend's father—whom she had only seen in photographs—standing beside her. He remained as an indistinct, floating spectre for a few seconds only, and before she could react, he vanished. The strange vision frightened her. While she was perfectly ready to forget it and relegate the apparition to the past, he visited her again, this time in a dream, the father's face alone hovering over her while she lay in bed.

Sometime around February of that year she had to return to her house twice in one week—two times between the biweekly visits of the maid. The maid had not been in the house between her visits and neither had the house been open to anyone. She checked with the maid and a friend who kept a key—neither had been there. She had been home only a few minutes when she noticed that the throw pillow which she personally had placed just-so on the sofa had been moved as if someone had sat there. She straightened the pillow, wondering how it could have been disturbed when no one had been in the house since she last straightened up. As she was leaving, her eyes were drawn to a side table in the foyer. She had used this table to display a favorite autographed book of hers, angling it carefully, centered on the table to her liking. The book had been moved to the side of the table.

A rational woman, she ran through all the possibilities in her mind: The maid had not visited during the time the items were re-arranged; the house had not been opened since she left; there had been no reports from the police that her security system, common to many of the homes in the area, had gone off. As she told me the story over the phone, I could almost hear the confusion in her voice.

One other thing she mentioned reluctantly. A woman who lived on another road nearby, several years ago, had committed suicide. It was rumored that she had been seen since, in the neighborhood, and even in some of the houses along her street, returning to the places where she had once attended cocktail parties with Gettysburg's local residents. It was almost as if my friend did not want to ask: could it be the troubled spirit of the woman who had returned to somehow help with the housekeeping while she was gone?

My friend returned home to Gettysburg again after another week of travel. One of the things she had been concentrating on during that week was a personal collection of her late husband's artifacts. She herself was not interested in keeping the large collection. In spare moments that first week in March, she had given much thought as to what she would do with the private arms collection.

On the site where a couple hundred thousand military weapons played such a large part in the lives—and deaths—of thousands of men, her thoughts of a few artifacts, it would seem, should be insignificant. Or were they trying to tell her something, these poor boys so horribly marred and mutilated who once lay so close to where the house now stands, whose reluctant spirits were set free by the types of weapons she now spent so much time and energy on....

She was sound asleep one night. Awakened by a strange light coming from outside her bedroom door, she arose and walked to the hall and down the stairs. She noticed that the foyer light, which she had turned off before retiring, was now aglow. Confusion turned to mild panic as she realized that perhaps someone had entered the house. But that was impossible with the security system she had. She turned off the light and returned to bed.

The next morning she left Gettysburg again.

About a week and a half later she took her husband's collection to a local dealer to be sold. In a week she was back in Gettysburg. I received a phone call from her about 9:45 p.m. Her voice betrayed her. She was agitated and frightened.

She had gone into the basement to find something and returned upstairs. A little while later she needed to go into the basement again. While in the basement she noticed that the shutters on the window, which she always kept closed and which she was sure were closed less than an hour before, were open. I tried to calm her over the phone, but she was rattled and continued to talk about how she never, never opens the shutters, and she was 99% certain that they were closed the first time she went down to the basement. Then she asked me a question that made me shudder: "Do you think it's in here with me now?"

I tried to calm her. I assured her that of all the stories of supernatural beings I have collected, I knew of only one that was malevolent. That may have not been the right thing to say. I am sure she was thinking that hers could be the second.

She said one last thing before we hung up: She had noticed, in her lovely, pristine home, the door to her guest room was scuffed and damaged, as if someone had kicked at it.

Bright and early the next morning my phone rang. She sounded distraught and exhausted. She had slept very little. The strange things had continued through the night.

While upstairs in her bedroom on the telephone, from downstairs came the distinct sound of the door to her basement closing with a solid and unmistakable "thunk." (I have examined the door to the basement—that is exactly the sound it makes. As well, the door is weighted so that, once opened, unless it is pushed completely back to the wall, it closes by itself, with that distinctive "thunk.") A little nervously, she told her caller that she had to go. She hung up and went downstairs. The door to the basement—the one she had just heard close—was wide open.

Around 10:15 that night, she had gone downstairs to get a drink. As she passed the dining room, she noticed that one half of the louvered doors between the living room and the dining room—a door she has always kept closed—was open.

Things seemed to quiet down for a little while until springtime. Hospital Woods changed from a dull mud color to pale green and the scrub redbud, whose ancestors were once watered with the blood of brave men, blossomed with their own pink flowers. The abundant dogwood, said to display each Easter the iron-red Stigmata in the four corners of its bloom, reminded some people of other great sacrifices made on this very ground to set men free in a more secular way.

It was a lovely evening during the first week in May. My friend had an audio tape on the player in her bedroom. The tape played until the end. She turned the tape over, listened to that side, then turned off the tape player and went to sleep. At 2:30 a.m. she was startled awake by the tape playing. Somehow it had been rewound and started at the beginning of the side she had heard last. She got up and turned off the machine. As a last gesture, she unplugged it.

I received a FAX at 11:15 on the night of June 1. My friend could not get through since I was on the telephone line. The FAX reads: "I just discovered some unusual things—3 nail holes driven in my desk in the foyer; the book moved again; and the grandfather's clock just chimed 12:00. I reset it back one hour—now it is working well! I love this house!!"

I talked to her the next morning. She was in a much better mood than the last time we had spoken. She almost seemed resigned to the fact that she was going to have to live with whatever it was that co-occupied the house with her. She told me that when she went downstairs that morning the drapes in the kitchen were open, yet she had closed them the night before. As well, the door from the dining room into the living room—the same one she had seen open before which she always kept closed—had been opened again. She also had gone out into the garage and found her car cover, which she had always carefully stretched out and folded, rolled up in a ball on the garage floor.

Things quieted down again through the summer and fall. We continued to have phone conversations whenever she was in town. For a while I thought that the soldiers from thirteen decades ago who had wandered through the physical space now occupied by this modern home had settled down. And the neighbor who had answered in her own way Hamlet's question, "To be, or not to be?" had finally found peace.

But I got another phone call from the woman the next time she was in Gettysburg. In her travels, she had consulted a clairvoyant. The clairvoyant, knowing little about my friend's past, in their session saw inside of my friend's Gettysburg home. Indeed, she said, she had seen three distinct forms meandering aimlessly through the house. Surprisingly, she saw my friend's husband; she saw the figure of the woman from down the street who had long ago committed suicide; and she saw out of the corner of her mind's eye, moving swiftly and quietly along the floor near the baseboard, the image of my friend's cat, dead too for several years.

These mental images of the clairvoyant could be relegated to simple good guesswork or perhaps mere coincidence—for those of you who believe there is such a thing as coincidence. But she identified each so well, so distinctly to my friend, that there could be no mistake as to who they were....

My friend then told me how, when she had first gone upstairs she saw something strangely out of place. Her husband's heavy bureau had been pulled out, away from the wall. Normally it would have taken a couple of strong men to move it; surely the maid could not have done it by herself. Questioning the maid confirmed that fact.

Next, she went into what used to be her husband's bathroom. There, in the sink, were remnants of toothpaste, as if someone had recently practiced oral hygiene and forgot to wash out the sink.

A little frightened, but even more perplexed, she returned downstairs to calm herself. Instead of relief, she found one more piece of evidence left from the Otherworld: on the chair where her husband used to sit, and where her cat liked to lounge, as if it were some strange gift across the rift between life and death, were scattered tufts of white cat hair.

With that the story should end. But it does not.

While following up on my original notes on this story, I called my friend—as I do with all my sources for stories of the paranormal—to clarify some details in order to flesh out the story. She had not told me that anything unusual had happened in the house since the end of my original research. As I was asking details about the toothpaste left in her late husband's sink, she commented, "Yes, and in the guest room too."

"What?" I said. "Something happened in the guest room?"

"Yes," she replied. "The same thing. This last time when I came home. It was as if someone had used that sink and forgot to clean up."

"And the bureau, too," she added, almost nonchalantly.

"What about the bureau?"

"It was moved. You know how it was always centered between the windows? When I came back this last time, it had been moved about six or seven inches to the right."

It would have taken a very strong man—or a couple of soldiers, Civil War variety—to move that heavy bureau. But with the same ease with which they traverse time and space, they apparently can, as well, alter *our* own surroundings at their whim, even in the sanctity of our secure homes.

THE QUICK AND THE DEAD

It is an unwise man who thinks that what has changed is dead.

—Anonymous

Devil's Den is closely associated historically with the Triangular Field. The fighting men of the North and the South who swept through the Triangular Field ended up in the tangle of boulders with the older and more sinister name, whether they were advancing or retreating. While Devil's Den received its name either before or shortly after the battle, the Triangular Field was named within the last twenty years. While studying aerial photographs of the Devil's Den area, some historian in the National Park Service noticed the oddly shaped field. Most of the prosaic Pennsylvania Dutch farmers who first farmed the land plowed back and forth, piling the stones that their plow hit onto a wooden sled drawn behind the plow. The sled was dragged to the edge of the field and the stones were piled there, hence the stone walls still seen about the battlefield, first placed to rid the fields of rock, then used for three killing days in July 1863 as protection. For the most part, the walls have not been moved since the farmers first built them; then the soldiers reinforced them for protection, and then the Civilian Conservation Corps preserved them in the 1930s. So the Triangular Field, in spite of the collapse of the lower wall, has retained its character since the battle.

It apparently has retained other characters as well.

If you study "ghost" activity, you realize that, for the most part, it is harmless. The truly nasty ghosts are really merely pranksters, moving things to inconvenience or annoy us mortals, roaming around our houses, creaking the floor boards above our heads with their footsteps, and making some of our favorite and most reliable modern mechanical devices fail unexplainably and usually only temporarily.

Cameras of all types occasionally fail, or jam, or rewind automatically, or flash by themselves, while in the Triangular Field. Reviewing the letters I have received, over the last two years since *Ghosts of Gettysburg III* was released, I count five cameras and four video cameras that have been reported malfunctioning while in the Triangular Field. It may have been more frequent than that: mine was a cursory survey, and not everyone writes to tell me about their camera going on the blink in the Triangular Field since it is not marked as such and they may not know where they were when the camera went haywire.

In addition, my mini-survey does not even include the large number of strange photos people sent me that were taken within the three-sided field. These show everything from bizarre faces, to misty groups of apparent soldiers trotting across the field, to the odd shrinking of the subject of one photo from a full sized adult to a childlike figure.

One is tempted to blame it on whatever mysticism the trinity has held in our civilization. Three-sided objects have always held a fascination for the human mind: Pyramids; The Bermuda Triangle, also known as the Devil's Triangle; The Trinity: Father, Son, and Holy Ghost. Could being enclosed in a three-sided space have an effect upon whatever is within? Some mystics will swear....

Mysticism has its place. But I was interested in a possible scientific explanation. It came inadvertently.

Dale Kaczmarek is the founder of the Ghost Research Society based in Illinois. He and his wife were in Gettysburg a couple of years ago just passing through. Dale called and graciously invited me to lunch to discuss our common interest. It was an enjoyable conversation, although I must always defer to others who are more knowledgeable about the paranormal aspects of my studies. I am a writer, historian and collector of paranormal tales, not so much an "explainer" as an observer. I seek out patterns in the stories I have collected which may reveal additional information about the phenomena. Beyond that, I begin to feel uncomfortable.

As the lunch hour ended, Dale began quizzing me about this "Triangular Field" on the battlefield. I related a few of the many stories I have collected about the place. I ended with the lament that I have always wished I had some scientific instruments to sweep the field and see if there were any physical anomalies out there, like perhaps a lodestone buried there or an over-abundance of iron in the soil to create electromagnetic fields that play havoc with the sensitive electronics in modern cameras.

Dale looked at me and said, "I have those instruments in the trunk of my car!"

The trip to the Triangular Field seemed to take longer than usual. We parked the car across from the gate and Dale opened his trunk. Inside was a large metal camera case. He opened it and began to remove instruments from its padded interior. I was handed a geiger counter; Dale carried two other instruments and his wife carried two more. Included were a gaussmeter to detect electromagnetic fields, a static electricity detector and two other devices to detect physical anomalies.

We swept the field. We probably spent 30 to 45 minutes moving about with our instruments as I told Dale and his wife the history of the site. The whole time there he detected only one small spike in the static electricity detector that he held. According to him, it was not much.

In other words, the Triangular Field, scientifically, is as normal a field as any cow pasture in the world, as normal as your own back yard. I left the Triangular

Field that day satisfied that I had ruled out one source for the cameras playing tricks out there. The only problem was, I had eliminated the logical, down-to-earth, scientific explanation for the problem. That left another less than logical explanation....

❖   ❖   ❖

Shortly after I met with Dale, I got a call from Joe Farrell who lives near Gettysburg. He is a self-described amateur "dowser." Dowsers, if you remember back to your grandparents' day, used certain natural instruments—branches from trees, metal wire—to discover unseen, underground sources of water. In the early days, dowsing was indeed a practical and reliable method of finding not only water, but other substances below the surface of the earth. Joe was interested in bringing a friend of his, master dowser Cecil Downing to Gettysburg and, in particular, to the Triangular Field. In a recent conversation, Joe had discovered that Cecil realized that his dowsing skills not only helped him to discover water—he has over 800 successful wells to his credit—but also sources of energy, possibly electromagnetic or gravitational, but definitely sources of residual human emotional energy. Cecil believes he can pinpoint this energy as belonging to either groups of people or individuals. His theory was that, in finding the residual emotional energy of groups, he could possibly locate where battlelines were; with individuals, he might be able to determine at what spot on this earthly plane, one single individual may have experienced the most emotional event any of us will experience: one's own death.

Joe had a couple of his own theories he wanted to test. Through my books, he was aware of the repeated failure of modern photographic equipment within the unusually-shaped field. He visited the Pennsylvania Bureau of Topographic and Geologic Survey in Harrisburg to inquire about the makeup of the geology upon which the battlefield of Gettysburg rests. He wondered if the crystal structure of the rock at the Triangular Field could have anything to do with its effect upon electronic equipment, or perhaps, if magnetic emanations through fissures in the bedrock could cause sensitive equipment failures. A resident geologist at the bureau said diabase rock did not fracture so as to conduct the earth's natural magnetism. Perhaps that is why the sensitive instruments that Dale Kacsmarek took into the field registered nothing.

One of the things Cecil can do is locate sources of water, or even sources of residual emotional energy, by "map dowsing"—using a small pendulum on a string hanging over a map of the subject area. (I have seen him do this, and it is quite interesting: The pendulum seems to move in a circle at certain spots on the map. The movement abruptly ceases when the pendulum is moved to another spot. If Cecil is somehow affecting the movement of the pendulum, he is doing it in defiance of Newton's laws of motion.)

I supplied the maps of the Triangular Field and Joe and Cecil worked with them prior to visiting and dowsing at the Triangular Field. By map dowsing, Cecil located several areas he wanted to field test for residual emotional energy.

The Triangular Field.

I met Cecil and Joe at the Triangular Field along with a friend and former park ranger Paula Fink. I took along my Sharp Viewcam to record the event. Ironically, the Viewcam performed perfectly the whole day.

In an interview prior to Cecil's dowsing session, he mentioned that he had been to other sites on the battlefield. At some locations, he said, you cannot hold the dowsing rod level even when trying. It is drawn to the ground violently. One such site was Iverson's Pits. Later, although he said that similar sites were all over the battlefield, he mentioned one other area where he could not hold the rod up: "Over on the other side [of Little Round Top] where the Maine men stopped them." The famous battle site of the 20th Maine where Col. Joshua Chamberlain ordered a bayonet charge when their ammunition ran out.

He also mentioned that the dowsing rods were merely an extension of his subconscious mind.

As we walked just outside the Triangular Field, Joe mentioned that natural fissures in underlying rock in fields will sometimes provide lines of easy movement for "discarnates and entities." These lines are called, in Shamanistic tradition, "spirit paths." Joe wondered if somehow the energies are sometimes captured by those lay lines, and are destined to remain within those confines for an extended period of time.

Cecil first worked the area along the wall outside the Triangular Field. He found lines that he thought were not associated with the American Civil War battle there—perhaps indicative of the remnant emotions of a prehistoric indigenous people or Native Americans, a conclusion arrived at by at least two psychics who had visited the general area before.

We entered the Triangular Field. Cecil found at least four areas and several lines where the dowsing rod dipped toward the ground. There is a large, flat rock with scrub trees growing around it that seemed to be a center from which several lines emanated, all going in the same direction toward the stone wall, but stopping at the wall and going no further.

After moving through the field for 20 to 30 minutes, he stopped and mentioned that at the flat rock there could be a particularly strong energy field. He also postulated that perhaps, on that spot, a squad or group of men were stationed who knew "their time was up." If the men were killed at the time when their emotions were running high, their energy could remain in that vicinity.

We moved from the bottom of the field, up the hill to the top where the gate in the rock wall is located. Cecil stopped at least twice, and with his arms indicated a general area of no more than fifteen or twenty feet around where he said mysteriously, "something happened here." The first area was roughly where historical maps indicate the 124th New York made its stand after its ill-fated charge into the Triangular Field, where it lost its colonel, A. Van Horne Ellis and its major, James Cromwell. The second area he indicated was just a few yards in front of the gate to the field, the spot where I was standing both times when expensive, professional network video cameras failed. "Something happened here," he indicated with his arms.

Suddenly Cecil exited the Triangular Field and followed his dowsing rod to the corner of the field nearest the gate. He seemed almost agitated as he walked to that corner. Unbeknownst to Cecil, that was the corner that psychic Karyol Kirkpatrick had pointed out, saying that she felt in that area there had been much blood and death; she said she felt that the trees were actually weeping because there was so much more than they could absorb and asked if, at one time, there had been a hospital on that site.[1]

"Something happened right in this corner, right there," he said. "I can't explain it. Very high emotions; that's about as close as I can come."

Earlier Cecil had mentioned his theory about human emotions: We give off electrical energy when our emotions run high, and give off extremely high energy levels when we die. Cecil has found that in murder cases, if the deceased had enough time to think about what was happening, he can pick up the residual energy of the individual's dying. Joe postulated, from what he has read about monolithic sites around the world, that they are often constructed with granite, that particular mineral having the appropriate crystalline structure to give it the ability to amplify or retain human emotional energy. I might have thought this pretty far out thinking if not for the watch I wear on my wrist with a quartz crystal in it that vibrates rhythmically to the tiniest amount of electrical energy given off by a battery smaller than my fingernail.

We moved over to the corner made by two sides of the triangular wall. Cecil dowsed just outside that corner and found an area of particularly strong residual energy. Joe pointed to the three largest trees on that spot and noted how they seemed to be growing away from where Cecil's dowsing rod dipped to the earth. Paula was particularly interested and walked over to the spot between the three trees. She smiled and motioned for me to come over. She pointed up. "Notice anything unusual about these trees?" she asked.

Sure enough, looking up through the three trees that angled away from Cecil's spot as if repulsed by whatever negative energy had been left there, I could see that nearly all the branches on the trees were growing along the side of their trunks away from the spot, radiating outward from the center.

Whatever happened on that spot just outside the Triangular Field was perhaps just as emotionally traumatic as what happened inside. Could even the trees, as Karyol once suggested, be indicating revulsion at the most heinous sin of fratricide?

❖   ❖   ❖

It is true that many famous people are really very nice. That certainly is the case with Mary Saladna, a television anchor from WGAL in Lancaster, Pennsylvania. One of the assignments the anchors have is to come up with a three part special on some local item of interest. Mary called to ask if she could do her special on my *Ghosts of Gettysburg* series of books. Of course I said yes.

We spent a couple of days shooting on-site interviews and background shots in August 1995. On one of the hottest days of the month we were out at the Triangular Field preparing to shoot a recreation of an event that happened to another camera crew. What we got on film was an actual paranormal event.

I had told Mary about the film crew from Harrisburg who had come to Gettysburg just before Halloween about a dozen years ago. The event is described in *Ghosts of Gettysburg*. It revolves around the fact that, as I was about to tell my story—in front of their video camera—of the many camera failures that have occured in the Triangular Field, their $12,000 professional video camera failed for the first and only time in the year-and-a-half they had been working with it. They had to apologize to their TV audience for the low quality of the video they brought back from the Triangular Field. *Something about a spirit angered at photographers for once dragging his mortal remains around to pose him for a picture....*

Mary's plan was to call in the original crew with their original equipment and have us recreate the scene of their camera failure so that she could show her audience what had happened. She made some phone calls and got the original crew from twelve years ago to come to Gettysburg. They even found the original camera that had given them all the trouble.

John Jones, a highly professional, talented videographer with whom I have worked on a number of video projects was the director for the original crew. He and his crew and Mary and her crew were arranging things at the gate entrance to the field. I was standing up on the road through Devil's Den, trying to stay cool in the shade. I was there for just a few minutes watching them set up when

Mary came walking up the hill to the road where I was standing and handed me two video tapes which they had shot earlier.

"Could you hold these?" she said. "Something weird is going on down there. I don't know if there's a magnetic field or what, but I don't want the tapes we've already shot to be ruined. Thanks," she said, turned right around and walked back to her crew. I stood there with the tapes in my hand. Slowly I began to smile.

In spite of Mary's fears, somehow I knew that nothing was going to happen to the tapes they had already shot, so I began to walk slowly down the hill to that once horrifying, oddly-shaped field. I virtually followed in the footsteps of the 124th New York as they made their forlorn assault into the field. When I got down to the camera crews, confusion reigned.

The original crew was setting up their equipment so that they could film Mary's crew filming them for their archives. The cameraman had the video camera all set to go, but the battery pack he wore around his waist suddenly went dead. He had removed it and was trying the second of three that they had fully charged earlier that day. It too provided power for just a few seconds before it went down. They were trying the third pack and were having trouble with that when Mary realized that they might be having a paranormal experience right before their camera.

You can see in Mary's tape the scene looking away from the Triangular Field, looking up the hill towards Devil's Den. You can see Mary's hands gesticulating in the foreground as she realizes what is happening behind her cameraman. Her cameraman begins to turn his camera into the Triangular Field and you can see John Jones' men working on their battery packs...but only for a second or two.

Suddenly and without warning, Mary's tape shows wavy lines, then severe interference that completely blanks out the picture. No more tape was made that day at the Triangular Field.

Later, I asked her what had happened. In her words, "it was almost as if the camera had taken on a life of its own." The camera would speed up, then slow down unexplainably. She told me that there was no reason for it to do that. There is a digital readout in the back of the camera; if anything is going wrong, the camera does a self-diagnosis and shows a sequence of numbers which correspond to numbers in the manual that tell what is wrong and how to fix it. She said the readout was giving them nonsense numbers, sequences that had no meaning to them and had no connection with anything that could go wrong with the camera. Reluctantly the two camera crews packed up their equipment and left the Triangular Field.

During the Civil War it was often the sign of victory when one side or the other retained possession of the field after the battle. In the Victorian prose of the Civil War era, you often read of the number of men a unit "left on the field of battle." Perhaps some remain to this day. Regardless of who won the battle of the Triangular Field on July 2, 1863, today the victors are the possessive dead who have remained to protect the terrain they fought and died to gain.

FATE'S CHILDREN

Imperious Caesar, dead and turned to clay,
Might stop a hole to keep the wind away.
O, that that earth, which kept the world in awe,
Should patch a wall to expel the winter's flaw!
                              —Hamlet, Act V, scene i.

Being a carriage trimmer and dealer, Andrew Woods had little call to get his hands dirty with the woodwork and the blacksmithing needed to produce the fine carriages for which Gettysburg had become known. Yet the men who did that kind of work frequented his small shop and two-story brick home on Breckenridge and Baltimore Streets. There were a few men he worked with: Mr. Hoffman and his young assistant Wesley Culp—who, he had heard, had joined the Rebel army after Hoffman had taken his business southward to Virginia—and that Studebaker fellow from a few miles north, the one who had the crazy dreams about a carriage propelled without a horse. Well, just because they were good workers did not mean they all had good sense.

But when they came, usually on Tuesdays, Thursdays and Saturdays, it was with the pieces of carriage they needed to have trimmed out—the seat frames, the steps, the tops—and it seemed never-ending. Up to the door they marched, hands full with their parts. In the recent good times Woods thought he might wear the old door off the hinges opening it and closing it for the heavily-laden workmen.

But they would not come this Thursday. Not with the Rebel army in Gettysburg, in his very house. He could hear them upstairs, moving to the second floor where their "sharpshooters"—as they called them—could fire out the windows at the Federals out Baltimore Street on the hill where the cemetery stood. Things would quiet down for a while, then suddenly, "Crack!" and a musket would pop with a ball of bright fire. If he peeked out of the cellar, definitely a dangerous thing to do, he could see the fireball and feel the concussion of air, and hear the whistle of the ball as it flew down the hill. Some Northern soldier had already found the range back to his home and took a chunk of the salmon-colored brick out with a bullet right near his upstairs window.

Out on the street the Rebels had built a barricade across Baltimore Street right at Breckenridge so that they could fire down the street at the

Union troops. Yesterday they had brought their wounded back from the fighting west and north of town. He had seen them take the mangled and maimed soldiers into the Pierce house across Breckenridge Street. Woods was glad little Tillie Pierce had gone out the Taneytown Road to escape the town; what seeing the horrors he had seen being carried into her house would have done to the sensitive girl, the Lord only knew. Apparently, the same use was being made of Henry Comfort's home just above him on Baltimore Street. And now, he heard his own door open and close, open and close; opened by the bloody hands of orderlies for men with their hands full carrying the helpless wounded, and closed again by those same helping hands.

Again he heard the old door above his head open and close. All day and into the night, over and over, until the sound of helpful hands assisting the helpless nearly drove him mad....

In January 1997, *Ghosts of Gettysburg Candlelight Walking Tours*™ purchased the lovely Civil War house at 271 Baltimore Street, on the corner of Baltimore and Breckenridge Streets. Renovations were made and the house was opened as a headquarters for the tours as well as a sales center for selected Gettysburg-related items. Of course, one of the more frequently asked questions about the house is, "Are there any ghosts here?"

Careful analysis of the 190-plus stories—both published and unpublished-collected for the *Ghosts of Gettysburg* book series shows that one of the patterns

Historic Andrew Woods House,
the Ghosts of Gettysburg Candlelight Walking Tours*™ *Headquarters.

that has emerged is that every time the physical status quo of a historic site is altered, there seems to be an increased amount of paranormal activity. In February and March 1997, the house was being renovated from its previous incarnation as residential apartments to the reception center, offices and headquarters of *Ghosts of Gettysburg Candlelight Walking Tours™*. I was at the house virtually every day to answer the carpenters' questions, decide on lighting or pick paint colors. I spent many hours in the upstairs offices, painting, adding chair-rail and cleaning. One set of cabinet doors in the Civil War section of the house—old beaded doors to a storage space just under the stairs to the attic—seemed to come open when I was gone. I started making sure they were closed whenever I left the house, fastening the little swinging latch every time. I was almost disappointed when, upon returning to the house and walking through the offices, I would find the cabinet doors still closed. When I would come back and they were open, I was more curious than frightened. I would close them again and feel for a breeze. That section of the house dates back to the 1830s. Surely there was a draft coming from somewhere to blow the doors open, but to unhook the latch would take a clever breeze indeed....

But reason must reign. Evidence must be documented. More eyewitnesses must be procured and unexplainable events must be able to be repeated in a laboratory. Otherwise this normally ordered world descends into chaos and we become nothing more than Fate's children tossed upon the Seas of Random Chance....

Maggie Hollis is manager of the tours. She is a solid young woman, much more apt to examine a situation logically, figure it thoroughly through in her mind, then come to a rational conclusion. That is why she is working for the company. That, and the fact that her entire family, from great-grandparents on down to the present generation, have an impeccable reputation for absolute honesty. So it was with all that in mind that I listened to her as she told me of how she was standing behind the information desk, talking with a visitor, when suddenly, above their heads and between them, a bright ball of energy—some sort of flash of light—loomed and burst with a popping or cracking sound. Both saw it. It had happened just moments before I got into the room. The shock and incredulous looks were still on their faces as they explained to me what happened.

I have seen this "ball of energy" before. It appears in some of the scores of "ghost" photographs people have sent to me, sometimes bright white, often green or greenish-blue. It is one of the more convincing pieces of evidence of some sort of energy which is momentary, subtle and sometimes visible to the naked eye.

Finally, one unusually warm February morning, I was discussing some construction details with our carpenter. As we finished our discussion and I was about to leave he asked me, with just a hint of a smile on his face, "Do you believe in ghosts?"

Example of an "energy sphere" in the Triangular Field.

Photo by Rick Fisher, PA Ghost Hunters Society

I smiled and told him what I tell everyone: That I believe that something goes on after this life; that death is not a closing door, but one that is opening; that we humans cannot now, nor probably never will, be able to explain everything; and that I believe that the people who have told me their stories about their paranormal experiences were telling me the truth. Then I added, "Why?"

"I only believe in what I can see or touch," he began. "I don't know about ghosts, but...."

I had to encourage him: "Did something happen here, at this house?"

"Well," he began. "I was out here on the porch cutting trim. The inside door to the kitchen was open and the storm door was closed on my electrical cord." He was pointing to the door leading into the oldest part of the house—Mr. Woods' carriage trim shop. "I had picked up all the pieces and, of course, had them in the wrong hand to reach for the door handle. I was shifting them to my other hand so I could open the door, when, all of a sudden, the door swung open. I walked inside, turned to close the door, and it swung closed."

My polite smile began to fade as I mentally inventoried all the other doors and windows in the house. No. It had just warmed up this morning; no other doors or windows in the house were open to cause a draft and it was not a particularly windy day. But I had to ask: "Was the wind blowing—could the wind have opened the door?"

"I thought about that at first. But it has happened three more times since then. In fact," he said, "the third time I had my hands full, I called to my

47

partner, 'Hey, Tom—watch this!' I walked toward the door and it opened by itself—he saw it—I walked inside and the door closed. And it happened one more time after that."

It was then that I told him that a carriage trimmer had once owned the house and that that particular door led into what was once his workshop. "Well," he said. "I guess it was just one worker helping out another. We do that all the time."

Yes, I thought. But it is a very loyal guild that lends a helping hand across that other more ominous and permanent door that Death guards.

A few weeks later I was taking one of my oldest friends in Gettysburg on a tour through the house. She has had paranormal experiences in her own historic house and is psychically sensitive to entities or presences. We had gone around the downstairs and had passed through the upstairs offices. We were standing at the top of the stairs when she got a strange smile on her face. She obviously was not listening to what I was saying. She held up a finger, said, "Wait a second," and walked into the middle room—what was to become my office. She came back out smiling even more broadly. "There's someone in there," she said of the unoccupied and darkened room. I said nothing. I knew exactly what she meant.

Halloween, of course, is when we have the most fun at the *Ghosts of Gettysburg Candlelight Walking Tours*™. The tours are extra busy and our customers often dress up for them, so we have quite a collection of interesting "beings" on the tours. Media coverage in Gettysburg is extensive, which informs people that we really do have things to do here *after* Labor Day.

Virtually every year Jim Cooke, a local radio DeeJay calls to broadcast with Karyol Kirkpatrick, psychic, live from a historic venue in Gettysburg. In 1997 we brought Karyol to the Ghost Tour headquarters. Although we had the history of the house that was admirably done by local historian Elwood Christ for the borough's Historic Buildings Survey, and thus possessed the documented history of the house, I was interested in the undocumented history which only Karyol seems to be able to provide.

So much has happened on this planet, on this earth that has gone unrecorded. And here at Gettysburg, with nearly 175,000 human souls packed into the few square miles surrounding the town all under mortal terror for their very existences, no historian born or yet to be born, can or ever will unearth everything, every word, every gesture, every movement that was made. Perhaps that is where one with special gifts can be of help to us concerning events of the past. Like the novelist or poet or prophet who helps us understand our lives by interpreting them for us, there are others among us, gifted ones who can see other things besides just those which have been recorded on paper....

We were scheduled to tour General Lee's Headquarters—The Widow Thompson House at Larson's Motel—and the surrounding area with Karyol

48

starting at 6:00 a.m., October 31. However, Jim wanted to record her impressions of the Civil War era house at 271 Baltimore Street for play on the air. So a week before the live broadcast, the radio crew came to the "Ghost Headquarters."

Karyol began, as she always does, moving about the house by herself, following where "the energies," as she calls them, take her. Sometimes she records her immediate impressions on a mini-tape recorder; sometimes she just makes mental notes for later use. She went through the house, then returned. She led us to the oldest section of the house. We began our journey there.

We entered what is now the kitchen area for the first floor. The modern kitchen occupied the section that was built in 1834. While in the room, Karyol mentioned the name Mary, who loves cooking: Karyol smelled mince pie. She also got the name James, and heard someone talking incessantly about God.

She moved immediately to the corner of the kitchen near the door to the outside and stated unequivocally that there was a spirit that stays in that corner, in the closet area. That, of course, is directly behind the door that was opened by some unseen hand for our carpenter. Karyol knew nothing of the carpenter's experience. In fact, she asked if the kitchen area was part of the original house.

She also asked if there was an "under area." Karyol got impressions of something being brewed. (This is a common impression she gets in older houses. No doubt that is because most people in the nineteenth century made their own beer or wine.) She got the impression that there may have been at one time, black market or secretive dealings going on underneath the oldest part of the house. Only certain people knew about it. "The name 'Mary' comes up," she said again.

We descended into the cellar of the oldest part of the house. Once in the damp darkness, she asked if a couple of men hid in there. As we came down the stairs she "saw injured persons and blood." There was no direct documentation on the house that said it was used as a hospital, but the Pierce House on the opposite corner of Breckenridge Street and the Comfort House adjoining to the north on Baltimore Street were both documented as having sheltered wounded men. One can only assume that Andrew Woods' home was used as well.

She also said that there were three major families that used the house over its long existence.

We went to the cellar on the other side of the dividing wall between the 1834 section and the 1837 section of the house. There she heard music and instruments. She got the distinct impression of men from Georgia and Virginia in the house and couriers coming and going. (Although there are no records to support the presence of Virginia troops in the house, Brigadier General George Doles' Georgia Brigade held the town of Gettysburg, with its main line running east and west along Middle Street.[1] Physical evidence backed up by written documentation places skirmishers at least to the Schriver House, one half block south of the Woods House on Baltimore Street.)

Karyol saw a woman in dark clothing: She "acted" like she did not "have it all together," apparently as a ruse. According to Karyol, she had a mission as a clandestine courier and was very good at it since everyone thought she was crazy and paid her no attention.

Karyol felt that a man had died in the house, but, "he's okay. You may hear some tappings in the house every once in a while. That's him."

Then she said something that reminded me of an experience a young man had while working for me that past summer. He was in the middle upstairs room, which serves as my office. He had been working on something while sitting on the floor. He described how, when he stood up, he felt something heavy across his shoulders that he seemed to be forced to carry until he walked out of that room. I asked him what it felt like. "You know what it feels like when you're carrying a little kid across your shoulders? That was the feeling."

Karyol said that a child had died upstairs, but he still plays there sometimes. "You may hear the rolling of marbles across the floor." "But Karyol," I said. "There's carpet on the floor." She smiled and said, "That doesn't matter. You'll still hear marbles on the wood floor."

She felt the presence of a man who "professed to be religious. He may slam doors."

We ascended the stairs to the second floor. There she heard the sound of a woman's voice calling the name "Charles," and received the name Mary again, or perhaps Marie. She saw the shutters to the window closed, the soft glow of candlelight, and men sleeping on the floor of the upstairs rooms. (This made sense. The upstairs windows of the house were used by Rebel sharpshooters and, at night they closed the shutters and lit candles so as not to draw fire from Union pickets on Cemetery Hill. No doubt, having found a safe place with solid brick walls, they were happy to spend the night there.)

As we descended the stairs Karyol again reminded us of "Mary," and said that she comes and goes, and if we ever hear things like leaves rustling outside when there is no wind, it is just her spirit passing by.

Re-reading the "official" history of the house reminded me of Karyol's uncanny ability to come up with names and events that are directly linked with whatever site she is exploring. Karyol said she felt someone in the house's past talked a lot about God. According to the deed, the land was once owned by the Reverend Alexander Dobbin, one of Gettysburg's earliest landowners. One of her first impressions as she was in the oldest section of the house was of a man named James. The Reverend Dobbin's son James bought the land from his father. According to Woody Christ's history of the house, Confederate sharpshooters used the upstairs windows to fire upon the enemy. There was a Mary Kitzmiller associated with the house at one time and her son William died in the house. Strangely, she had another son whose name was Charles.

While in the kitchen area—the oldest part of the house—a beeper worn by one of Jim Cooke's co-workers continued to buzz, but each time she tried to see who had paged her, there was no page. Jim Cooke's tape recorder began to run slower while he was in the kitchen. He thought the batteries were getting low, but when he left the room, the tape resumed its normal speed. He returned to the kitchen and the tape slowed; out of the kitchen it ran fine.

And finally, one of our employees was in the house watching the desk for customers as we traipsed around the house. She is devoutly religious and has a healthy skepticism about the spirit world and the existence of ghosts. While our group was upstairs, Mary—that is her name, just like the Mary that Karyol mentioned—heard the loud slam of a heavy wooden door in the old part of the house. She was confused because she knew that no one had opened that door yet that day. She investigated and found the door shut. She checked the door and indeed it was closed tightly. Perhaps, she thought, someone had inadvertently opened it by mistake. She returned to the information desk. Suddenly, from the Civil War section of the house came the unmistakable "slam" of the door once again.

The houses that we are born in, live in, eat in, worry in, love in, and die in are very much like the physical bodies we are given in which we do all those same things. And when our physical bodies die, our essences leave, like animals that moult and leave merely the shell of their forms, to move on to a new and greater unknown adventure.

NOTES FROM THE OTHERWORLD

Be thou a spirit of health or goblin damn'd,
Bring with thee airs from heaven or blasts from hell,
Be thy intents wicked or charitable,
Thou comest in such a questionable shape....
—Hamlet, Act I, scene iv.

In the sullen, inexorable tramp of time and all of vast eternity, the Battle of Gettysburg could have been fought just yesterday. In fact, looking at Earth on July 1, 2, and 3 from a distant star, say 134 light-years away, the Great Conflict is just now occurring. If some intelligent creature on a planet circling that star had a telescope powerful enough to see the details of Earth, would he be able to see the desperate struggles on McPherson's Ridge and through the Railroad Cut? Would the Confederate lines surging up Little Round Top and Culp's Hill be discernible? And could that gross capitulation of souls we call Pickett's Charge even be noticed at that distance? Probably not.

Yes, the great battles that break a hundred-thousand mothers' hearts and destroy families and alter genetic lines forever, from some places in this universe, cannot even be seen. The smoke and haze and fire are invisible. But the All is changed, from God's point of view.

Perhaps that is why we try to memorialize the venues of Death. But making a battlefield into a manicured national park with monuments and administrators may be the worst thing anyone could do—it trivializes the horror and sanitizes the disgusting butchery that war really is. Preserving these killing grounds should be mandatory. But, as William Manchester noted, turning battlefields into recreational areas "may be an attempt to exorcise the desperate past," meant to benefit the morbid curiosity or abject guilt of the living rather than memorialize the dead.

He chose his words wisely. Perturbed spirits, restless souls, and the essences of men exist and seem to need a helping hand to flee their tortured lives on that spot where they died. As Shakespeare wrote, "I am afeared there are few die well that die in battle...." Many deny that there are ghosts at Gettysburg—or anywhere on earth—and that may ring true to those who have never experienced an unexplainable event. But the argument is hollow to those who have.

I have been asked if I have ever "seen a ghost." I can say with assurance that it is one thing to collect reports on hundreds of supernatural occurrences involving the mysteriously unexplainable. It is a completely different thing to experience one....

In the afternoon of July 1, 1863, the Union line, which had formed a rough, upside-down "L" west and north of Gettysburg during the fighting, begins to collapse. The lines north of town begin their retreat as pressure from Jones's Confederate artillery battalion to the east of Barlow's Knoll increases. A withdrawal is a perilous thing at any time; under fire it is particularly delicate.

Retreating from their position on Barlow's Knoll, hundreds of men pass an ominous portent—Potter's Field, the graveyard for the Adams County Poorhouse, the buildings of which are several hundred yards closer to town.

The broad fields between the knoll and the buildings would become a killing ground for thousands of converging Confederates if they reached Barlow's Knoll and got organized before the Union men crossed it. Some men of distinction did not make it across.

Brigadier-General Francis Barlow, only twenty-nine years old, takes a bullet in the side, then a spent ball in the back as he tries vainly to walk back with his retreating lines. He lies down to rest.

Since that day, some parts of the field of retreat behind the Union lines have been altered. Consider Carlisle Street, for example. Seventeen acres on the west side were dramatically altered—extended, flattened and graded for playing fields by Gettysburg College. Behind the houses on the east side of Carlisle Street, the land is still pretty much the way the soldiers who rushed over it saw it—albeit under so much stress that they likely took little note. At night, a walk across this field is full of those little noises and things seen out of the corner of the eye. Things that disappear after they have left their trademark goosebumps.

A bullet passes through Barlow's hat and another grazes his finger. Before he is taken off the field, he is nearly killed by his own artillery. Incredibly, he survives the battle and the war.

My dog, as a puppy, refused after dark to walk down the alley behind my house which leads to these former fields of conflict and avenues of fear and death.

Nineteen-year old Lieutenant Bayard Wilkeson, commanding a battery on the bloody field is struck by a shell which kills his horse and leaves his right leg dangling by the sinews. He finds that his mangled leg impedes his crawl back to the shelter of the Poorhouse....

One night, I had just returned from a meeting. I pulled into the alley that runs behind the houses on Carlisle Street and began to descend the first of two small swales when the headlights on my van illuminated something in the distance near my garage. At first, since the thing I was seeing seemed to shimmer slightly, I thought it was a reflection from one of the pools of water that lay in the roadway. The closer I got, the more solid it appeared until it had seemingly coalesced into an upright column. The mind plays odd games when confronted with the unexplainable.

...and so Wilkeson takes his own pocket pen-knife, cuts the remaining tendons, and crawls away from his own leg.

My first thought was not that it was "a ghost," but rather, a reflection. As it coalesced, I remember thinking, "A dog—no—too large." Then I thought, "A deer—no—too upright." Finally, as it grew into a column and began to resemble something familiar in my mind's eye, I thought, "Prowler!" and stepped on the accelerator.

Finally finding succor in the poorhouse buildings, thirsty beyond imagining, Wilkeson is brought some water. A nearby wounded soldier begs, "For God's sake, give me some."

I had been about a hundred yards from it when I first saw it. As I closed on the silvery column, it seemed to stop for just an instant. I noticed that it was incomplete; about the height of a man, it floated, suspended in the air, a foot or so off the ground. The prowler apparently noticed my now-speeding van, although I could not discern it turning and looking toward me—it just seemed to stop. Perhaps it was already turned toward me; perhaps it just sensed me.

Young Wilkeson passes the canteen, from which the other soldier drinks every drop. Before another canteen can be procured, the young Samaritan dies. His own father, a correspondent covering the battle for the New York Times, has the horrid duty of reporting on his own son's demise.

Suddenly it moved—no, floated, for I saw no legs or means of propulsion beneath it—from right to left across the alley and into an enclosed cul-de-sac formed by my garage and my neighbor's on two sides, and my six-foot tall fence along the back. I was not more than twenty yards from it as it moved at a rather quick pace into the trap. I immediately pulled my van in after it, swinging in a wide arc so that my lights would cover the area enclosed by the garages and the fence. (The fence's framework, by the way, is along the inside of the structure for aesthetic reasons. The fence is smooth along the outside and it would take an incredible athlete to vault over it between the time I saw the apparition move into the cul-de-sac and when my lights brightened the fence.) I squeezed the van as close as I could to the fence to illuminate the area behind my small shed. Nothing.

Men who were wounded in the first day's fight lie dying in battalions. They have been since early morning, so what is one death among hundreds...unless, of course, it is your own. Those who find the courage stand for a while in the open fields north of town and in the town itself, then retreat; those with overpowering instincts for self-preservation run; those with feelings in between walk when they are under observation or are tired, and run and skulk when they can get away with it.

I backed out of the area, keeping my lights trained on the only path of exit. I quickly put the van in the garage and pushed the button to lower the garage door while I scoped-out my fenced yard.   No one there.   No one had set off the motion sensor light in my back yard.   My dog had not barked.   I hurried to the garage door windows and waited for anyone to come out into the brightness of the spotlight above the garage door.   One...two...five minutes.   Surely I had out-waited any frightened prowler who would have the advantage by sprinting out into the darkened, former battlefields behind my house before I could summon the police....

Literally thousands of frightened, desperate boys run and stumble southward to the east and west of the Carlisle Pike, across the gully that drains the fields and into the northern end of town.   Not poor, young, brave Bayard Wilkeson. He would never run again.

But there is no out-waiting Eternity.

THE BRIDGE TO NOWHERE

...so now for these brave spirits who held together for manhood's sake in the name of what they already felt to be a doomed Confederacy. Virginia was but a prison-pen; the Southside Railroad was the dead-line; the river the Lethean stream. There was blood at every bridge and ford....

—Major General Joshua Chamberlain

The United States Naval Academy in Annapolis, Maryland used to teach America's future naval commanders that rivers were in-roads into the heart of the enemy's territory and great highways upon which to bring unlimited supplies for continuance of the fighting. The United States Military Academy at West Point, New York taught its future generals that rivers were impediments: fine places to anchor a flank so that no enemy could get at it, and even better in front as a broad, flat killing ground where the assault troops must expose themselves without cover to wade across, or funnel themselves into a tightly packed column to cross a bridge, vulnerable to concentrated fire from small arms and artillery.

U. S. Grant probably used the rivers as no other Army man thought to. Perhaps learning much from his 1863 Vicksburg Campaign about the use of the Mississippi, he went to the eastern theater of the war and utilized the Potomac, the Chesapeake Bay, the James and the Rappahannock Rivers unlike any of his predecessors had. He claimed that the reason for establishing his base at City Point, Virginia, at the confluence of the James and Appomattox Rivers, was because the wounded from the upcoming battles would travel easier on boats back to Washington. His humanitarianism notwithstanding, the rivers also gave him an unlimited supply of weapons, ammunition, rations, and that most vital matériel for war, fresh soldiers.

But rivers and streams played an important part in other battles throughout the war, as the names of some of them reflect: Bull Run; Stone's River; Pittsburg Landing (on the Tennessee River). Even the Union armies were named after the great rivers in the war theaters they occupied: The Army of the Potomac; The Army of the James; The Army of the Tennessee.

If it had not been for the prominence of the town, the Battle of Gettysburg might just as easily have gone down in history as the Battle of Marsh Creek since a number of tributaries that drain the area in which the battle was fought flood into that stream. The first day's fight might just as well have been called the Battle of Willoughby Run; the second day either the Battle of Plum Run across which the Confederates attacked on July 2, or the Battle of Rock Creek, since that was the stream below Culp's Hill. If Meade had pulled out of the battle on the night of July 2, the ensuing battle might have been called the Battle of Pipe Creek. That was where he had planned his fall-back position if things did not go well.

So the creeks and streams played an important part even in this land-locked Battle of Gettysburg. Though most of them in the battle zone were not formidible enough to affect tactical plans, they still provided water for the men, both healthy and hurt. Those who were wounded and crawled to them for life-giving refreshment, left the waters tainted with their own life's blood. Those paralyzed by wounds who could not move away from the creeks and streams, found themselves facing desperate, panicked, final moments as the waters rose after the rains of July 4, and slowly engulfed them in Eternity. And there is at least one ghost story that pre-dates the battle about a prominent local creek that the old settlers used to tell.

Young, vivacious Peggy Noel was on her way back home. From what or where, we do not know. Perhaps a dance held out of town. Perhaps a late night soiree with some handsome beau. Wags would have her in some illicit affair, but there is scant evidence of even the story itself: just the name, Peggy Noel, and the horror of a late night accident involving the buggy she was riding in. It happened, apparently at the bridge on the Fairfield Road that crosses Marsh Creek, for that is where she has been seen at certain times ever since. The accident was high speed—horses and a buggy completely out of control—and involved a shearing or slicing, perhaps by one of the thin, iron-hooped wheels. The details, again, are sketchy. But there was a decapitation.

Over the years, in the spring, when the trout run and the fishermen are wading Marsh Creek at feeding time in the dusk, they sometimes hear a rhythmic splashing, sounding very much like another fisherman wading towards them. They are annoyed: Why doesn't he walk along the bank instead of scaring the fish away? And the fish do flee before the wading feet. The angler looks up, not to see a burly fellow fisherman, but the wispy body of a young girl. Now the fish are not the only ones to flee, for as his eyes move up the torso the fisherman realizes that there is no face to accompany the body. And there is no face because there is no head. And the woman cannot walk out of the water, because, with no head, or face, or eyes, if her feet leave the familiar stream, she will be lost and wandering the earth forever.[1]

And at least one crossing of Marsh Creek at Gettysburg played an emotional, heartholding role for both some Union and Confederate soldiers. Apparently, the creek still holds at least one other soul captive.

Sachs Covered Bridge, over Marsh Creek, was built in 1852 by David S. Stoner. In engineering parlance, it is a latticed truss bridge, the criss-cross design of which gives it a solid, unmovable look. One hundred feet long, it

Sachs Covered Bridge over Marsh Creek.

spans Marsh Creek just above the old dam. For years the lovely bridge carried nothing more sinister than some farmer's grain to market, or lifted some flock of sheep over the waters below.

But during the Battle of Gettysburg the Sachs Bridge helped to transport men and arms of both armies. On July 1, 1863, Doubleday's Division of John Reynold's First Corps used the bridge to get to the battlefield; Biddle's and Stone's infantry brigades and the artillery pieces of Cooper's Battery also crossed that fateful morning. Late that evening, Humphrey's Division of Dan Sickles' Third Corps used the bridge.

But to hundreds of men in Longstreet's and Hill's Confederate Corps, it was not Marsh Creek they crossed, but the River Styx, in a one-way, no-return sojourn. If you remember your Greek mythology, it is across the Styx that all human spirits must ultimately travel, ushered by the last ferryman, Charon. Across Marsh Creek lay 97,000 Charons, with the name, "The Army of the Potomac," all waiting to point the Confederates the way to the Land of Nevermore.

On the second day of the battle, the bridge ended up in the rear of the Confederate lines and remained in their possession until their retreat on the night of July 4 and early morning hours of July 5. Because of the abundance of water from Marsh Creek, the area around the bridge was used for a Confederate encampment, pasture for the thousands of cattle and horses that accompanied the Southern army, and hospital and burial sites.[2]

After the Civil War the bridge returned to its pastoral role, again serving the farmers and travelers of Adams County, Pennsylvania. The bridge was closed to automobile traffic after 1968. It suffered severe flood damage in 1996 having been washed completely off its buttresses. But with the help of many local businesses, non-profit organizations, and state grants, what has been called the most historic bridge in Pennsylvania was restored. It has been known as the romantic setting for many a youthful tryst, as well as a terrific fishing hole for local anglers. Occasionally a tourist will find his or her way out there and have the opportunity to be transported not just across Marsh Creek but apparently back to another time.

Douglas Dziama from Ohio has been a Civil War enthusiast from his youth. I should know. He is my first cousin and he and I used to travel to Gettysburg with my parents when we were children to wander the fields in awe. Together, we became even more awestruck as our knowledge grew of the battle that changed so much world history, and much of the personal history of some 175,000 men and boys who struggled there.

He is more familiar with the American Civil War and the Battle of Gettysburg than most average visitors to the area. Being a businessman, he is also more levelheaded and objective than most. That is why his and his family's experience at Sachs Covered Bridge is remarkable.

It was a day in early August when he and his family drove out to Sachs Covered Bridge. Although he had known that it existed, he had never been to the unique site and he wanted to share it with his wife and two daughters. Having just seen the movie *Bridges of Madison County* he thought this would be an opportunity to combine his newly piqued interest in covered bridges with his study of sites associated with the Civil War.

He pulled his car up to the western entrance of the bridge. The eastern entrance had been closed for a number of years with the condemnation of an old iron bridge. The current eastern approach is circuitous, difficult to find, cuts along a farm lane and is long and arduous to travel. Theirs was the only vehicle at either end of the bridge. He described the scene in a letter:

> We got out of the car and walked up to the west end of the bridge. We noticed the creaky-wooden planking of the bridge roadway, the lattice-covered sides, and the grafitti on the inside and outside walls. But what we all noticed at the other end of the bridge was something that remains a mystery to this day.

It must be remembered that for many of the nearly 175,000 who fought, suffered and died in the Battle of Gettysburg, it would become one of, if not the most important part of their lives. It surely, through hindsight, was for most of them, the closest they would ever come to crossing that very real bridge into Eternity.

Many returned to visit the place where they had almost died. Some came back repeatedly to see the spot where they came so close to the other world they could have reached out and grabbed it. They brought wives and friends and relatives; they brought their sons so they could show them where they had touched the Fire. They returned for the several reunions, especially the twenty-fifth in 1888, and the fiftieth in 1913. And, a mere 1,800 who were left of those two magnificent armies brought into existence for the sole purpose of annihilating one another, returned for the seventy-fifth reunion in 1938.

At other times they listened to their former officers speak at Gettysburg when they returned for the dedications of their regimental monuments. Some listened to Maj. Gen. Joshua L. Chamberlain as he spoke of the dead:

Now you have gathered these bodies here...You station them on the ground they held. Here they will remain, not buried but transfigured forms,—part of the earth they glorified,—part also of the glory that is to be....[3]

The veterans wandered all over the battlefield on their return, from East Cavalry Field, three miles east of town to Hunterstown and Fairfield and Hanover where they also fought. They returned in carriages and on crutches and canes, and in wheelchairs, men whose time had come when they were young, who endured for their cause and country, and who returned to look at it again as if it were all a dream or a vision....

Doug continued his narration:

For you see, sitting in what was an apparent wheelchair was the slouching figure of an old man; a man that seemed out of his element, like a fish out of water. His wheelchair was facing in an easterly direction, like he had attempted to cross it. He was not fishing from the bridge because he was not facing the water. His image was silhouetted and dark. He wore a large floppy hat.

At first, I thought it was probably an old man taking a nap. But how did he get here? He would have had to power himself with his bare hands the distance of one-half of a mile from the main highway to get to the bridge. There was no one around who could have taken him there.

In a subsequent conversation, I asked him if he had seen a car across the bridge. It is possible—but very difficult—for people to find their way to that side of the bridge by auto. No, he answered. There was no car on the opposite side of the bridge.

As I gazed across the bridge, one thing became brutally clear to me: that we were gazing at an inanimate figure; one that did not appear to be breathing; one that did not even appear to be among the living. My gut feeling was that he must be dead, for he made no effort at moving....

Later, without prompting them on what he had witnessed, he had his daughters write down what they had seen. The comparisons are interesting. First, his oldest daughter Susan:

I remember looking across the bridge and seeing a person in what appeared to be a "stroller," similar to the ones used in malls. This man was slouched in his seat and lay so still that I did not notice any movement. He seemed almost too big for the "stroller"....

She remembered him wearing "an old-looking shirt," and some sort of a cap instead of a hat.

Jennifer, Doug's youngest daughter, recalled a little more:

The image was a man in a wheelchair, and it's still clear in my mind. He was an older man, probably in his late 50s early 60s. He was slouched down in a wheelchair and his head just appeared to be hanging from the base of his neck pointing towards his right shoulder. Although he looked like a man, there was some sort of inhuman attribute about him. He was almost scarecrow like in nature, and he was wearing a flannel shirt....

Jennifer also remembered a cap. The rest of her narrative is rather chilling:

He was completely still, and he didn't even breathe. I remember his arms and how they hung lifeless from his body about midway down the wheels of the wheelchair; they looked as if they were composed of stuffing or straw and not of flesh. This man, this image seemed so lost and out of place....it didn't make sense...it looked as if there was no access to the bridge by anyone who attempted it. This made the man's location even more uncanny. He was completely alone, without another soul in sight and he lacked a purpose. There could be no explanation as to why he was on the bridge, or how he got there. Standing on the opposite side of the bridge watching this man, I couldn't shake the feeling that something was not right. The eerie feeling that overwhelmed was indescribable. A part of me was curious and wanted to get closer to the man, but I could only bring myself to walk halfway down the bridge; something held me back....

Jennifer was not the only one who had a sense of death and forboding. Doug at first agreed with his daughter that perhaps they should cross the bridge to investigate. But at the last second Doug suddenly heard a voice inside his head shout a warning: "Leave this place, NOW!" The rest of the family apparently felt the same. Without much discussion, the entire family got into the car and drove away.

They told me about the experience later that evening at dinner. The next morning I accompanied them to the bridge. We inspected the area where they saw the "image" of the man, as both Jennifer and Doug continued to refer to him in their written reports. There was no evidence that there had ever been a man in a wheelchair there—no empty cans, no cigarette butts, and, most distressingly, no wheelchair tracks in the soft dirt and gravel road that leads from that end of the bridge to the arduous route back to...wherever he had come from.

...We left for Ohio shortly after and wondered. Was the man discovered by authorities and taken to a homeless shelter, or, perhaps a morgue? Surely if the man had died on the bridge, it would have been a leading story on the front page of the local newspaper. And Mark would have read about it and called us, wouldn't he? Two or three days passed; Mark never called.

When the bridge was replaced after the 1996 flood—well over a year since the time Doug and his family were treated to their "image"—far thinking planners had installed one convenience on that side of the bridge for the time when the area becomes a public park (government budgets willing). There, just below where the "image" sat unmoving is a modern concrete ramp for those in wheelchairs to use.

Instead, we are left to wonder to this day, who was the mysterious old man in the wheelchair? How did he get there? Was he perhaps a traveler in time, attempting to cross a timeless chasm? I suspect we will never know....

DEATH'S HIGH HOLIDAY

Because I could not stop for Death,
He kindly stopped for me—
The Carriage held but just Ourselves
And Immortality.

—Emily Dickinson, 1863

The National Park Service estimates that approximately 1.7 million people visit Gettysburg during the year, most of them during the summer months. Visitation is especially high during the traditional holidays: Memorial Day, the Fourth of July (which coincides with the anniversary of the battle) and Labor Day. The question is often asked, Is there any particular time when there seems to be more paranormal events than others? The answer is that it seems that there is more activity around the anniversary of the battle than at other times. But one must wonder: Is that a function of the activity of the spirits during that particularly traumatic (for them in their previous incarnations) time period—the time of their own wounding or death; or is it because there are more people around to witness anything paranormal that would occur "normally" anyway? In other words, are the spirits just as active all year round, out in the darkened fields of battle, but there is just no one there to witness their cavortings?

Everyone expects to see ghosts out on the "battlefield"—meaning what the National Park Service owns. Remember that the government owns only a fraction of the "battlefield," and that the real battlefield encompasses the town of Gettysburg, the Pennsylvania (now Gettysburg) College campus, the Lutheran Theological Seminary grounds, the Evergreen Cemetery, as well as numerous privately owned in-holdings and the hundreds of properties adjacent to the park boundary where troops lounged and bled, ate, slept and died in agony.

Imagine, (or perhaps actually witness!) on some sultry summer night out along the dark road from Baltimore, the heaving, panting, undulating column of men, (or what appears to be the entity of a column) known once in this world as the Union Army's Sixth Corps, in a ghostly reenactment of their terrible 34 mile forced march.[1] Eighteen thousand souls under arms stretching ten miles along the roads, marching the quickstep and taking three hours to pass a given point.

And what is that we hear wafting through the summer night? The bands keep playing through the long night march and the march of the next day: "John Brown's Body," and its refrain by Mrs. Stowe, "Glory!

Glory! Hallelujah! His Soul is Marching On," taken up by a hundred, then a thousand, then the entire corps, through this last night on earth for many. And another song: It is the haunting melody of *"Home Sweet Home,"* sung most heartily by the boys of the 93rd Pennsylvania as they cross the Mason Dixon line.[2] Many are indeed going home, home to the Father and His mansion with many rooms. Are they forced to repeat this horrible march—again and again and again—as reparation for their participation in the world's most ancient sin—brother killing brother—committed those three days in July 1863?

Or, if we are in the right place near Frederick, Md., at the right time, will we see an apparitional rider dismount in front of a hazy tent to deliver, yet again after all these decades, the order to Maj. Gen. George Gordon Meade informing him that he has been given the command, virtually within sight of the enemy on its most threatening invasion, of the Union Army? Will we see on the pale wraith's face, the look of anguish as the fate of the souls of 97,000 men is placed in his hand? If his ghostly face could look into the future, would he change his mind if he could see the 51,000 casualties his decisions will cause?

And out the road to Cashtown, at the old inn there, if the conditions are just right, can we see through the hazy mist that gathers in the South Mountain passes, the curious faces that sometimes peer out the windows at those taking photos of the ancient building? When we enter the structure that Robert E. Lee once entered along with dozens of others wearing stars on their gray collars, can we hear the clinking bottles as they re-filled the officers' flasks to fortify them for the butcher's work of the morrow?

If we want to see all of the "battlefield" we must certainly include those sites fought over by the far-ranging cavalry. For the infantry and the artillery, Gettysburg was basically a three-day battle, July 1, 2, and 3. But for the cavalry, there were battles that started on June 9 and lasted until the Confederate Army re-crossed the Potomac at Falling Waters on July 14, 1863. To appreciate the scope of the Battle of Gettysburg we must visit the area around Emmitsburg, Md., and also the Pipe Creek area where Meade had designed his fall-back position. Remember to see East Cavalry Field, Hunterstown, Hanover, and Carlisle. Journey to Maryland and visit Union Mills and Westminster and Rockville. And do not forget the mountain passes below Thurmont and the battlefields near Hagerstown and Williamsport and Falling Waters.

So indeed the killing fields are wide and long and numerous, right up to the very doorsteps in the little town of Gettysburg.

In June 1994, *Ghosts of Gettysburg Candlelight Walking Tours*™ began. In addition to telling the ghost stories of the town and adjacent fields, the guides tell a good bit of history too. Some of our guides are Licensed Battlefield Guides and so enjoy the status that particular honor brings. Over the years the tours have been a source of enjoyment for both visitors and guides. In addition, having guides roaming the streets of Gettysburg leading groups of interested seekers of the paranormal has given them much exposure to any spirits that may still be roaming the streets.

One of our guides, who has been a reenactor for a number of years and is quite an expert on women's clothing of the Civil War period had an eerie experience at the Jennie Wade House. She had related the sad story of the fate of Jennie Wade, the only civilian to be killed in the three day maelstrom that was the battle, many times over the past two summers that she has been a guide. Although she had studied the history of Jennie Wade and had led tours past the house of her death, she had never been through the house on their self-guided tour. Of course, Jennie's sad and ironic tale is well known: Her boyfriend lying mortally wounded is visited by his boyhood chum from Gettysburg, Wesley Culp, now wearing a Confederate uniform. He gives Culp a dying message for Jennie; the message remains unknown to this day, for Fate cuts down Wesley before he gets a chance to deliver it, cuts him down on Culp's Hill on the family-owned farm practically within sight of the house where Jennie dies.

What a surprising meeting it must have been on the Other Shore, when the least expected of all, Jennie, showed up to meet her friend Wes and her dearest love Jack....[3]

One evening after the guide and her male friend had volunteered their time as reenactors at a historic site in Maryland, they returned to Gettysburg. Still in their Civil War period dress, they went to dinner, then decided to cap off the evening with a tour through the Jennie Wade House.

They listened to the taped narration in the kitchen area where twenty-year-old Jennie was killed; they walked upstairs, through the hole blown through the wall by a shell, through which Union soldiers had carried the lifeless body of Jennie Wade some thirteen decades before, then moved through the rest of the house and down into the cellar. She tells the tale best from this point:

We sat down on the first row of benches and looked at the mannequin laid out to represent Jennie's body and listened to the tape that continued the story. The others on our tour began to leave when Brian noticed the chain that separates the display from the visitors was beginning to move. It did not swing; it was slowly vibrating up and down. Knowing that the "ghost" was supposed to be that of Jennie's father, I started to think in my head, not saying anything out loud, it was a shame that Jennie died so young, and while we didn't know her, we were there to pay our respects and in no way meant anything disrespectful. As I finished these thoughts, the chain stopped vibrating.

Brian and I turned toward each other and began to discuss what had just happened and what each of us was thinking at the time. We ruled out the possibility the chain moved due to vibrations from the street or the upstairs traffic as the chain is anchored to two solid field stone pillars. As I turned back to face forward, my parasol bumped into the chain causing it to swing back and forth. I put out my hand to steady the chain and as I did so, I could feel a strong "current" going through it. I asked Brian to touch the chain to see if he felt what I did.

As he put his hand on the chain, within a few seconds a very visible change occurred in his appearance. His face drained of color, he looked gray, sad and depressed. His shoulders caved forward slightly and I would have to say he "drooped." He began to talk about Jennie almost as if he had known her. He talked about how young she was and what her plans would have been for the future. He talked about how much of life she had missed; her wedding; unborn children; family gatherings; and celebrations.

By now, I was concerned about what was happening to Brian. He had heard me tell the story of Jennie, he knew of the stories about her himself, but he had never reacted like this before. I asked him if he was all right, but he didn't seem to hear me and went on lamenting Jennie. I suggested we leave the cellar and go outside. I helped him to his feet and guided him to the stairs. As we reached the ground level, Brian shuddered, shivered a little and let out a strong sigh then asked, "What in the world was that?"

He told me it was as though someone had come to sit beside him and placed their hand on his shoulder. His shoulder and right side went cold and stayed that way until we were outside. He was visibly upset and concerned about what had just happened. As an explanation, I suggested perhaps Mr. Wade had sat next to Brian, touched his shoulder and put the thoughts into Brian's head to be spoken out loud. Brian then said, "Jennie's father is not the only one down there. They're all there! There's more than one."

We went to the museum office and reported what had occurred. The young ladies on duty told us they worked there for a couple of years and never had anything happen to them. They never saw the chain move or felt a presence in the cellar, although one young lady admitted she was afraid of the cellar and would never go down there.

Brian would like to go back and take flowers for Jennie. It's a very strong feeling he has to do so. Perhaps his is a thought presented by Mr. Wade. After all, he never got the chance to take Jennie flowers. I've asked Brian to wait awhile before we go back. Right now I'm not sure I'm ready to take part in this experience a second time. Just the thought that Mr. Wade waits for us to return...for Brian to return...is more than I want to consider.

A number of visitors to the Jennie Wade House have experienced other strange phenomena. The chain in the cellar, of course, has been a constant source of evidence for some sort of unexplained presence. Cameras have a tendency to act strangely—or not act at all—in and near the house. While working on the story of the moving chain in the Jennie Wade House for *More Ghosts of Gettysburg*, my very expensive Minolta SLR camera went "on the blink" and I had to finish shooting the photos in the book with my publisher's camera. Visitors to the Jennie Wade House have reported their cameras jamming, or, stranger yet, showing odd, spectral images, verified by some experts from the Pennsylvania Ghost Hunters Society as those of "ectoplasm," or the odd shapes spirit-energy takes on: globes of light floating surreally, or swirling vortices.

The guides' experiences were limited to concrete occurrences.

Wanting to videotape our guides for training purposes (so that they could watch themselves give their tours) I brought in my RCA video camera. Diana Loski, one of the off-duty guides (who is also an author) was kind enough to offer to tape the other guides. She came back halfway through the tour disappointed.

"I think your battery is dead," she said.

"That's impossible. I charged it for two hours just before I brought the camera down here."

The battery was the original one to the camera, only about a year old.

"How much of the tour did you get?" I asked.

She kind of smiled. "Well," she said, knowing the story of cameras failing in the vicinity of the house. "I got about half—until we got to the Jennie Wade House. All of a sudden the low battery light indicator came on. Then the camera just died."

"Died?" The battery was supposed to give at least a half hour or so more recording time after the low battery indicator came on.

"Well," I said. "I'm sorry you came in for nothing. I'll buy a new battery. Can you try it again next week?" We arranged for her to follow another tour later.

I bought a brand new battery and charged it right up to the time I was to take it in for her next tour taping session. Out went the camera with Diana. Forty-five minutes later Diana was back again. This time she was more excited than the last.

"What happened?" I asked.

"You won't believe this. Everything was taping just fine...until I got to the Jennie Wade House again. I got the weak battery symbol in the viewfinder again. Then the battery died again."

By now I was getting angry. Something—either of this world or out of it—was interfering with my business. Diana and I just looked at each other and shook our heads.

We arranged for her to try and tape the tour one more time. This time I figured I would eliminate the possibility that it was that particular camera. I had just purchased an 8 mm, Sharp Viewcam. I charged the battery fully before taking it out to give to Diana. Although the camera was not as sophisticated as the larger one, it did not take quite as much energy to run it. I remember Diana smiling at me and shaking her head as she left the office to follow the tour.

A little over a half hour later she was back. The camera had failed. The battery had failed. Where? In front of the Jennie Wade House.

Three tries. Two different cameras. Still no tape of our tour beyond the Jennie Wade House. It was the last time we tried. In the meantime, the Sharp Viewcam has worked well ever since. But the brand new battery on the RCA Camcorder still will not hold a charge for more than 15 minutes.

Other guides have had strange things happen to their candle lanterns in front of the house. The lanterns that they use are all hand made. Very fine craftsmanship goes into each one. They are for sale—and therefore examination—at the *Ghosts of Gettysburg Candlelight Walking Tours™* Headquarters on Baltimore Street. At least three of our guides have been startled, as they stood in front of the Jennie Wade House giving their talk, by the sudden popping of glass. As they look down at their lanterns they see one strangely fascinating phenomenon: one of the glass panes in the lantern is broken. Not shattered, mind you, but holed. One guide described it as looking like a bullet hole through the glass...then he realized what he had said and where he had been standing: at the Jennie Wade House, right between what was formerly the Union battle line near the top of Cemetery Hill, and the Confederate battle line in town, near Breckenridge Street, where the tour headquarters is located.

❖   ❖   ❖

It was July 4, 1997. I was in the National Civil War Wax Museum in Gettysburg signing my books and Diana Loski and her children came in. She was dressed in her Civil War era clothing and was immediately recognized by a family that was having their books signed: "Oh look, there's our guide from last night!"

The night before was July 3, of course, the anniversary of the last day of the Battle of Gettysburg. It was also the anniversary of the death of one James McCleary who was killed on East Cemetery Hill and buried in the Evergreen Cemetery, just a few hundred yards from where the Confederate shell exploded that took off McCleary's legs and one hand. The hand, by war's strange coincidence, landed upon the artillery lunette—a semi-circular mound built up in front of the cannons as meager protection for the gunners. Legend has it that on certain nights, through the summer night's mist, there can be seen the shadowy figure of a lone soldier hunting around the lunettes for...something beloved and missing now...forever.

Diana told me later that while she was telling the story of James McCleary, she noticed that the people on her left were listening but those on her right were not paying attention at all. Instead they were looking into the dusky fields of East Cemetery Hill, pointing and whispering to each other.

I said "Diana, I hear from these people that you had an experience on your tour last night." She looked at me quizzically and said, "What do you mean?" She seemed unaware that anything had happened.

The family chimed in to relate a story that was almost too fantastic to believe. "While you were talking about the guy who got blown up"—meaning James McCleary, wounded by artillery— "above the man on the horse"—meaning the equestrian statue of O. O. Howard, "there was a pillar of blue light, like blue sunlight. It lit up the statue," the family spokesman said. "You could see him plain as day, you could see the grass was green at the base of the statue; you could see the cannons. It was like broad daylight right in that little column." Diana then realized why the people on her tour were looking around. They had been trying to see where the light had come from.

They were looking to see if it was perhaps the moon just coming from behind a cloud—but this was the early evening tour—the moon was not out yet. They said it lasted for several seconds and then vanished. They thought it was a trick or a hoax. They went back to the statue the next day to see if there was a light at the base of the statue that someone could have turned on. "The strange thing was, that it didn't seem to come from any source—it seemed to be its own source." According to Diana, those were their exact words.

Diana, whose back was toward the monument, had missed the whole thing. The family had never said anything to her because they thought she had planned it. It was not until the confrontation at my booksigning that the family and Diana realized that they had been involved in a paranormal experience.

In an aside, Diana told me that she wonders if perhaps McCleary likes her because she spent time at his grave in the Evergreen Cemetery.

Diana has had another strange experience with blue lights in the same vicinity of the Jennie Wade House. During one tour, she stopped near the Jennie Wade House to tell the tale of historic irony, of friends' and lovers' best laid plans torn asunder by Fate. She had just finished telling the sad tale, when one of the visitors asked, "What are those blue lights coming from the cellar of the Jennie Wade House?" Diana had taken dozens of tours past the house and had never seen blue lights—or any lights for that matter—coming from the cellar of the house after the house was closed. Puzzled, she merely responded that she did not know.

The entire tour took turns looking through the crack in the cellar door. They saw a blinding blue light—like blue sunlight.

One of the visitors wondered out loud if perhaps a ghostly presence was manifesting itself in the strange cellar. Another visitor—obviously the more skeptical type—guffawed, and said that someone must have left a light on by accident. He bent low to peer through the windows into the subterranean space, and tried to see through the crack in the cellar doors down into the space adjacent to the makeshift mausoleum that once contained the mortal remains of one Mary Virginia Wade. Indeed he saw the blue light pulsing from the depths—but as to its source, even this most scientific of minds could find none.

Diana too, had her doubts. So the next day she called the owners of the Jennie Wade House. Did anyone ever forget and leave the lights on in the house after the place is closed? The manager replied, yes, every once in a while one of the help forgets and leaves the lights on. Has anyone left the lights on recently, like the other night? No, he replied. He did not think anyone had left the lights on in a while. Does the cellar have blue lights in it? There was a pause by the manager. No, he said. No blue lights in the cellar. It is dark down there. They need all the light they can get, so they use white lights.

To Diana's knowledge, whether forgetful help has been working or not, no blue lights have been seen since in the cellar that once witnessed the flight from her body of the spirit that on earth was called Jennie Wade.

When *Ghosts of Gettysburg Candlelight Walking Tours™* moved its head-quarters and offices to the Civil War era house at 271 Baltimore Street, it shortly became evident that we had inadvertently moved into the neighborhood of an old—and long gone—friend.

In recent years, more and more people have been strolling the streets of Gettysburg. Visitors—who never seemed to walk much of Gettysburg in the past—in particular have been taking the time to walk out of the Steinwehr Avenue area of Gettysburg into the residential area of Baltimore Street. It can be a very pleasant experience, for Gettysburg—especially in the warm sorcery of night—retains much of its quaint nineteenth century allure.

It has been documented that at least one veteran of the Civil War lived on the next block of Baltimore Street. He has been seen before—although only in shadow form—and has been associated with his incessant pipe smoking. Just as more recent visitors to Gettysburg have discovered the joys of walking the streets of the town, it would be most common for someone living in the era after the Civil War to take an evening stroll along the street where they lived. From evidence gathered quite inadvertently by some of the guides for *Ghosts of Gettysburg Candlelight Walking Tours™*, at least one of our strollers is definitely not of the current era, and is visiting from a place much farther away than that from which modern visitors come.

At least three of our guides during their tours have experienced the heavy, sweet scent of pipe tobacco when no smoker is around. Sometimes the guides smell nothing but notice several of their customers looking around and sniffing. When asked what they smell, the answer is, "pipe smoke," but no one is smoking a pipe. Other times, a few people will come up after their tour and tell the guide about smelling pipe tobacco smoke somewhere in the vicinity of Baltimore Street, and that it followed them through some of the tour. Two young people following Mollie kept smelling it and thought the scent was following her. They could stand it no longer. They finally asked her if perhaps she was carrying a lit pipe. Of course she was not. First, she does not smoke; second, it would be foolish to carry a lit pipe in the folds or pocket of her hoopskirt.

More often than not, when the pipe tobacco smell is around, only part of the tour will smell it and the rest will not, which is odd, because the strong, distinctive scent of a pipe is usually omnipresent. But if odd, it is also indicative of a paranormal experience wherein just those sensitive enough to pick up the sensory elements of the entity will do so, and others, though standing right next to them, will not.

Mollie has asked some of the people who have detected the pipe's fragrance to smell the candle in her lantern—no, no, they say, that is not the aroma. One man identified the odor as a particular type of tobacco his great-great grandfather enjoyed: black cavendish.

Once, she had a group behind the large sign in front of the Gettysburg Area Senior High School (now the Middle School) near the Alumni Park, when suddenly a large cloud of blue-gray smoke rose from the opposite side of the sign. Nearly all the guests on her tour saw it, along with Mollie, rising slowly into the scented night air. One curious (and courageous) tour customer trotted to the opposite side of the sign, expecting to see someone smoking a pipe. To his—and everyone's—astonishment, not a soul...let me re-phrase that: no person was there.

Finally, one night—apparently when everything needed was in perfect alignment—the ultimate unexplainable event occurred. Mollie had just finished her tour and was back at the offices. Standing near the sign at the front of the building giving her conclusion to the tour, she noticed the eyes of some of her tour participants looking to her side and growing wider. Suddenly one of them shouted, "Your dress! It's on fire!" Mollie turned as another guest screamed, checked her hoop skirt, which was not on fire, then turned back to the guests in confusion. In panicked tones, she heard them chattering, "It was smoke!" "No, mist!" "It was right there, standing behind you. It collapsed when we screamed!" "What in the world was it?" Mollie calmed them down enough to gather their impressions. It was, as one guest described it, and the others agreed, a "pillar of smoke." At first the guests thought that Mollie's lantern, which she had put on the ground next to her, had caught her dress on fire. The pillar of smoke seemed to be coming from near or behind her lantern, and when the people screamed, the pillar "collapsed," into a much smaller entity. Some thought they saw it move rapidly, down Breckenridge Street, retreating toward the west.

Statistics show that only about ten to twelve per cent of all paranormal experiences are visual; about sixty per cent are audio; but all the senses can be affected, including, of course, the sense of smell.

FIELDS OF SORROWS

O monstrous! O strange! we are haunted
—A Midsummer Night's Dream, Act III, scene i.

Throughout the town of Gettysburg, certain orders of beings call on us from a past—their past, our own past before we were born—does it matter?—to question even that most obvious of all mysteries: what is real; what is illusory?

That Gettysburg has a strong pull to those interested in its battle history is undeniable. Hundreds of thousands of those with ancestors who fought here return year after year to the place of final reckoning for Great-great-Grandfather. Some others, admittedly, come to Gettysburg to see where *they* endured some incredible emotional trauma—in what they believe was their previous incarnation. (Perhaps then, there is a kinship between those who died here and were allowed to move on to another physical life—this one—and those, for whatever reason, are stuck here as spirits only.) Hundreds of thousands more come to try to understand why it happened at all, this most heinous of mortal sins—fratricide—to the species with the most highly developed ability to communicate of all on earth—the only species as well that perpetrates organized genocide upon its own. These are indeed two seemingly incompatible opposites.

On Broadway on the north side of Gettysburg, there is a house that was built years after the battle. In fact, there was no "Broadway" at the time of the battle: just farm fields, a few farm houses, and a toll house or two. Not that it matters. As we have seen countless times before, merely being built upon battle land—and virtually every square foot in Gettysburg was criss-crossed by history—is criteria enough for it to become a haven for some tortured spirit not entirely at rest.

It is obvious that some unseen beings are definitely not of the Civil War era. Apparently Gettysburg clings not just to those who fought here, or who just curiously visit, but to those who merely lived here, who may have poured out some of their life's passion, in protecting the town from criminals or from disease; who lovingly taught at the several institutions here; or who merely lived out their day-to-day existence in Gettysburg.

Many of the houses on Broadway have been occupied by educators from the Lutheran Seminary or Gettysburg College. Some of the houses apparently still contain the spiritual remnants of those who dedicated their lives to the edification of others. Perhaps, true to their life's calling, they still attempt to teach us something even in death....

Broadway, Gettysburg PA.

The death of one of these educators made the house available to one of his children through the ancient law of primogeniture. The inheritor moved into the house and lived there for a number of months before selling the place where he grew up. He has related a number of stories that are not necessarily linked to his father, but possibly to another teacher who had lived in the house before.

One night as he was in the house alone, above his head, he heard the distinctive sound of soft, slippered footsteps on the attic stairs. As he recalled it he smiled slightly, and indicated that it was a sound he had heard numerous times before when his father would climb the attic stairs to retrieve some stored family heirloom or old book that had not been used in years.

On other occasions he recalled hearing an even more familiar sound, one that could have no other explanation than that of a positive, physical manifestation from the Otherworld. Often at night, when the house was deathly quiet, he would hear coming up the stairs to his bedroom, the familiar sound of footsteps on the front steps. This he knew because the footfalls hit just the right boards, and they creaked as they had for decades before as visitors to the house stepped upon them.

Then, at random times he would hear something he had heard from his childhood on Broadway in Gettysburg: The front door would open, then close with a solid "kachunk," as if, once more, the well-liked educator, after a day of imparting his own wisdom and the love of learning upon his students, had come home to his own haven.

❖　❖　❖

Again to Baltimore Street, where hordes of armed warriors spent the first days of July 1863 in the sweltering houses, either as live combatants, or as helpless, wounded bits of their former selves, or as the dead leftovers of uncaring and careless battle. As Shakespeare wrote:

> *As flies to wanton boys, are we to th' gods;*
> *They kill us for their sport.*

Through the once peaceful houses the soldiers wandered. Most accounts have them doing little damage; but everything is relative. To a soldier accustomed to seeing men's entrails strewn on the ground by a fragment of an artillery shell, tracking pounds of mud into a parlor, or breaking open a pantry with a musket butt, or dipping sugar from a crock with a bloodstained hand may not seem like much damage. But to a persnickety Pennsylvania Dutch housekeeper, such invasions are tantamount to homicide.

There are also accounts of interior walls being broken down so that sharpshooters would have easy access to other parts of the building and at least one account of malicious Southerners pouring molasses down some stairs and dusting it with feathers from a pillow. In the midst of such carnage as was the Battle of Gettysburg, these acts seem child's play.

But nonetheless, the soldiers' presence in the homes was noted by angry housewives, many of whom turned right around and cared lovingly for the broken men, or perhaps wrote their last letter home to mother or wife, or who may have wrapped them in their own bedclothes as a winding sheet for one who may have in the senselessness of war, damaged their lovely homes. And though the men themselves have long gone, one young witness living in a historic house on Baltimore Street is not quite so convinced.

The house dates back to 1843. The young witness was eleven years old at the time of the incident. Before you dismiss the encounter as a figment of some child's imagination, read her account and note the dispassion with which it is written, as one who has observed an unexplainable, but nevertheless real event:

> This is the story. Once I was walking in my upstairs hall. I looked into the den which was at one end of the hall. There is a room right next to it. In the den I saw a ghost. It was tall and white. But I did see some kind of uniformish thing under a sort of white sheet wrapped around it. I[t] slowly moved toward me. I turned around to [sic] because I didn't want to see it. As I was about to go down the stairs I turned back to see if it was still there. It had disappeared! I looked in the room right next to that room. I saw nothing. I ran down the stairs. It was Christmas around that time. I was going around turning off little electric Christmas candles that we had. They had been on all night and were hot. I told everyone my story. My sister went up to the den with me to "investigate." The one thing we noticed was a thing that almost proved there was a ghost. The electric candle was icy cold. The same candle I had turned off only seconds before.

That is my story...This is another piece of vital info. My house was built in 1843. I live on Baltimore Street. I am only 11. But I assure you I am not joking here....

In a recent telephone conversation she admitted that it was a little difficult to recall all the details, but she remembered that the "ghost didn't have any legs." (Remarkably, the only visual apparition I have ever had showed nothing underneath it—even though it moved—or floated—rapidly.) She said she was not scared. I asked her about the white sheet she had mentioned. She said it "looked kind of like a robe, sort of." I asked her if it might not have been her dad dressing up. She answered with a very emphatic, "No!" In fact, she denied that it could have been her dad again later in the conversation, and explained that it could not have been her father dressing up because the whole family was downstairs having breakfast. She recalled that the apparition really did not walk toward her as much as it walked toward the wall "and disappeared."

On to Chambersburg Street. Down this broad avenue on the late afternoon of July 1, 1863, ran the Union survivors from the cataclysm a mile to the west. Back they scampered, through the steep canyon sliced through Oak Ridge for a future railway, and down the bed prepared for the eventual laying of ties and tracks. Some ran down the long hill along the dusty road from the Lutheran Seminary to the square of Gettysburg, followed closely by pursuing Confederates. Some of them may have thought about the poor fellows of the 16th Maine, left behind as a rearguard. Even the lowest private knew what that meant: they must—and would— hold their position until captured or dead; there were no other choices. Indeed, even now as some survivors of the Federal First Corps retreated through the square, the men of the 16th Maine, heroes to the last, were tearing their own battle flag to bits and secreting them inside their uniforms so that the Confederates could not inflict the greatest ignominy upon the regiment: the capture of its flag.

If the Union soldiers could have seen to their north the rest of their line collapsing, perhaps they would have increased their speed, for just a few hundred yards to their left, as they faced into the town, their comrades of the Eleventh Corps were also falling back, from their tenuous position north of the College to the little knoll just to the west of the road to Harrisburg. Everything was crumbling, and rolling like a converging wave toward the center of Gettysburg. Any officer who remembered his Shakespeare—such as Bowdoin College graduate Maj. Gen. O. O. Howard, commander of the Eleventh Corps— might have recalled the bard's words, never more appropriate than at this moment: *Confusion now hath made his masterpiece!*

Tumbling back toward the high ground that they would soon discover had a cemetery on it, the men formed jumbled bunches in the streets and alleyways. A large number ran past some of the makeshift hospitals in the town—mostly the larger buildings like the churches or college structures. One church in particular was Christ Lutheran Church on Chambersburg Street. There, one of war's small tragedies was about to be played out.

The place had been filling with wounded since early morning, having been, according to one source, the first building in Gettysburg to be opened for a hospital. An artillery shell struck the roof during the first day's fight. Once again, Gregory Coco's superb work on the hospitals at Gettysburg quotes a citizen of the town, Mary McAllister:

> Every pew was full: some sitting, some lying, some leaning on others. They cut off arms and legs and threw them out of the windows.... There was a boy with seven of his fingers near off.... The surgeon came along (and) just took his knife and cut off the fingers and they just dropped down.[1]

Sadder still was the fate of one of God's chosen, Chaplain Horatio M. Howell from the 90th Pennsylvania. He had been in the church seeing after the spiritual needs of the wounded soldiers and had just left through the front door. Unfortunately he was wearing the shoulder boards of his position and had buckled on his light dress sword. He stood watching as the advanced skirmishers from the victorious Rebel army passed along Chambersburg Street, firing at almost anything that moved and wore blue.

A skirmisher approached just as Howell and a wounded soldier exited the church. The Confederate placed his foot upon the church steps, right where the memorial plaque to Howell now stands, and shouted up to what he thought was an officer, to surrender. Howell apparently attempted to explain that he was a non-combatant, but the nervous Confederate pulled the trigger and Howell died on the top step.

The steps of Christ Lutheran Church where Chaplain Howell was killed.

76

In October 1995, renowned psychic Karyol Kirkpatrick was in Gettysburg exploring the James Gettys Hotel as it was being renovated before it became the magnificent hotel it is today. Remarkably, she said that as she was about to descend the stairs into the cellar, where a former manager once had an encounter with a Confederate soldier—a century and a quarter after he had left Gettysburg[2]— as she opened the door to the cellar, she felt the spirits rush past her, like a strong wind, from the cellar. "They don't like having me around," was her casual comment. She also asked if there had been a fire in the building. No one, including a historian and the owners of the building could remember anything about a fire in the old hotel. Interestingly enough, when the restoration was starting and upstairs walls and ceilings were being torn down, there, behind everything, were charred rafters, the unmistakable evidence of a fire.

I was moving some things around in my van so that I could give Karyol and Carolyn Thomas a ride to our next stop, when Carolyn asked me if there was any other place on Chambersburg Street that I would like Karyol to visit.

I casually looked around and said, "How about Christ Lutheran Church across the street. Just make sure you take her along the side so she does not see the plaque." Karyol admittedly knows nothing about the Battle of Gettysburg, and does not care to know—she simply is not interested. Still, in situations when I am working with Karyol, I always make sure that she has no idea of where we are going before hand, so that skeptics of her talents cannot say that she studied the area ahead of time. Here was a perfect opportunity to "test" her.[3] The thought came into my mind spontaneously, and the incident of Chaplain Howell is relatively obscure.

I had Carolyn write down her experience with Karyol that night:

> I took Karyol Kirkpatrick over to the church across the street from Lord Nelson's and asked her if she could tell me anything about it. She closed her eyes and said that both Northern and Southern soldiers had used this church quite a bit.
>
> We then ascended the stairs, stopping after 4 or 5 steps, and I asked her if that was all she saw? She closed her eyes once more, then spoke of seeing a man of the cloth being shot here, and that his last thought before he died was one of complete surprise that he had been shot. She said that his death was an accident, and that they hadn't meant to shoot him...that they didn't know he was a religious man (priest) and that they couldn't tell from where they were that he wasn't a soldier. They were very upset that they had killed a man of the cloth. She stressed one or more times again that shooting the priest (or minister—whatever he was) was an accident.

On Carlisle Street north of Water Street are some lovely buildings, remarkable because of their unique architecture. One home was built during July and August in 1895 for Mr. John C. Lower. It represents a fine example of a Queen Anne style "cottage" (although its 25-room size belies that appellation.) Its basic design is in the shape of a cross, much the way cathedrals are designed, with a few additions to the basic design according to the very few owners this particular house has had. The current owners show remarkable sensitivity to the history of the house and its classical American architectural style.

The house serves as the current owner's residence. The upstairs has been rented to Gettysburg College women for a number of years. Various groups of them have reported to the permanent residents some unusual activity that may be traced back to one particularly caring spirit who refuses to acknowledge that her days of toil on this earth are over.

One night several years ago in the fall after they had just moved in, all four college roommates were upstairs in their respective rooms. One by one they heard something moving mysteriously around the living room. When they emerged to investigate who was flitting about, no living soul was found. This was just the beginning of a number of odd occurrences that happened to the first set of women who lived there.

One Saturday afternoon all of the roommates attended a football game together. When they returned they noticed that each of their perfume bottles had been moved around or "rearranged," as if someone were making their rooms neater. It was not the last time it happened.

One winter night all the roommates were in bed. For several minutes they heard footsteps stalking the hall. As the women peeked out into the hall they realized that no one had gotten out of bed until just then to investigate. Then

House on Carlisle Street where a servant still attends to her duties.

there was the latch to the attic door that was virtually rusted shut. One morning they found it unlocked, as if someone had carefully and silently worked it open overnight.

Another group of women who lived there and had heard about the strange happenings from previous inhabitants of the house decided to hold a "seance" one evening, presumably with a Ouija Board. The names that kept being revealed were "Joanne," and "Joanna Craig" and the fact that she had been a servant girl about 20 years old. The women always "felt" as if this entity was looking out for them. And indeed, some of the things that occurred or have been seen in the house seem to revolve around an entity that is a care-giver. For example, some doors were found bolted from the inside against unwanted intruders. A microwave oven turned on by itself as if someone were trying to cook a phantom meal for the girls. Television channels often changed while the remote was untouched. And the women often said they could feel someone in the room just watching over them.

One woman, sleeping in her room on a spring afternoon, awoke to the distinct sound of fingernails scratching on her pillow circling her head. As the scratching continued she heard someone whispering. She opened her eyes and it stopped. She closed her eyes and it started again. This happened over and over until she finally got frightened and called her roommate. Exactly what the whisperer was saying could never quite be discerned.

The resident of the house was sitting in her living room downstairs. The women upstairs were apparently studying since the house was quiet. Suddenly—and frighteningly—she heard the horrifying sound of a human body tumbling down the inside stairs. She thought one of the women had fallen and ran to see. She opened the door just as the tenants opened the upstairs door. They all had heard it, but there was no one at the bottom of the stairs.

One of the college roommates always slept with her door open. Numerous times she heard footsteps come down the hall, pass her door and continue on. Time and again this odd but easily recognizable noise made its way down the hall, past her open door, and to the end of the hall, while no source for the footfalls could be seen. One night she heard the familiar steps approach again. But this time, as they reached her door, they stopped. As the woman watched amazed, the door closed, as if someone unseen was ensuring her privacy.

While digging the foundation for the back steps, the owner found a stone that was obviously carved into a rectangular shape. It was in the way of his construction project, so he pried it from the earth and tossed it aside. It landed where it rests today, just inside the fence. Visible across the top of the stone is the carved name "Joanna Craig."

There may be one other presence in the house as well. Psychic Karyol Kirkpatrick, during one of her Halloween visits to Gettysburg for a local radio station, visited the Victorian house on Carlisle Street and gave numerous impressions of the house. Much of what she "was shown" about the house related to what the many college women had experienced. One thing she said confused everyone, including the resident who had done a great deal of research on the house. Karyol said she saw a man in the house with a sword—a military man. Of course we all thought of the battle, but the house was not built until 32 years after the fighting here ended. Karyol was adamant; she saw a man with a sword in the house.

The statement remained a mystery until the resident reopened the research package she had collected for the house. There, on the Historic Building Survey form completed by historians Elwood Christ and Dr. Walter L. Powell was some information on John C. Lower, the first owner who had the house built. He was born near Gettysburg in 1844. Further research indicated that he was a Civil War veteran, and that his unit was involved in the Gettysburg Campaign. Furthermore, the unit was the 21st Pennsylvania Cavalry. Cavalrymen carried, as their armament, a carbine, a pistol, and the *arme blanche*—the saber.

And finally, one of our guides, Diana Loski, and her daughter were returning to their car parked across from the house on Carlisle Street. Diana was getting into the driver's side when she noticed her daughter staring up at the attic window of the house. She had a half frightened, half quizzical look on her face. "I can see her, Mommy. But now she's gone."

Diana asked her what she had seen. The little girl described a woman with her hair up in a bun, with an old fashioned dress on and a brooch at her throat. She was in front of the window. Across a stand was a rug. It appeared for an instant that she was about to use a rug-beater on it. Then she disappeared.

Joanna Craig, the faithful, unsung servant who may have died in that house from a fall down the stairs—and may even be buried in an unknown grave under the new porch—may still work her weary days and nights caring for the young women she still adores in the house she loved in life. And perhaps she is still overseen by the former cavalryman who built the pleasant home on Carlisle Street and keeps her—forever—to her tasks.

THE FIRST DEATHS

After the first death, there is no other.

—Dylan Thomas

What a monstrous thing they had gotten themselves into. From the first few shots out on the road to Cashtown, to the almost casual popping of carbines, to the nearly steady roll of volleys just in the forenoon, to the final destruction of the Federal line by evening, the first day at Gettysburg was like some immense tornado, drawing men and horses and weaponry from miles about into the vortex, then spitting out broken weapons, broken horses, broken men in a giant debris cloud that others had to clean up.

At least one of the Confederate officers who broke Lee's intentions not to bring on a general engagement, would write later that he had gotten clearance from a superior, in spite of fresh intelligence that the Federals were near, to march into Gettysburg for, of all things, shoes.[1] Even if there had been shoes—or the fictional "shoe factory" that buffs continue to tout as the reason for the great catastrophe—they would turn out to be very expensive footwear indeed. One man's life is not worth a pair of shoes; over fifty thousand casualties for some sewn leather is obscene.

The battle would stretch through three fiery days in July and burn up nearly one third of the participants as dead, wounded or missing—read "deserted" or "captured" or "liquefied by a shell" for "missing." Even more frightening is the fact that the armies caused those casualties in even less time, because they did not fight for three days straight. There were lulls in the fighting, such as the night of the first day and into the morning and early afternoon of July 2. As well, there was a lull on the morning of July 3. So, about 51,000 casualties were inflicted in only about 23-24 hours of fighting. Simple division shows us that during the fighting there occurred about 2,217 casualties per hour; which translates into about 36 casualties per minute; which further devolves into one casualty every two seconds.

Try snapping your fingers once every two seconds for a whole day and night. Your fingers will cramp after about an hour or so; you will thirst over that time period, you will get hungry, and you will get tired. You will be in agony after a while, but you can always quit any time you want. But the soldiers did not stop getting killed or struck by the lead and iron. One by one, monotonously they clicked on, and on, and on: healthy boys suddenly wounded, wounded boys suddenly amputees, amputees suffering

81

and dying, and dead boys carried out to be piled up and later buried in grisly graves barely scratched into the surface of the earth. Twenty-four hours. One every two seconds....

The Confederate commander, Robert E. Lee, did not arrive on the battlefield until mid-afternoon. Initially he was perturbed at the sounds of pitched battle coming to him as he rode in from Cashtown. But arriving near the buildings of the Lutheran Theological Seminary, on the ridge upon which that institution dedicated to brotherly love stands, he saw the Federal line before him and to his left virtually in full retreat, collapsing, imploding as it were, into the little village below. His mood must have changed at that moment from anger at having his orders not to engage disobeyed, to satisfaction that his men were obviously winning the battle he had not wanted to fight.

All around him was evidence of the sacrifices his men had made to secure the ridge he now stood on as well as evidence of the tenacity the enemy displayed in attempting to hold it. He may have heard that his men had killed a Federal major general—Reynolds, shot in the back of the neck within sight of the small stone house on the ridge.

One of the best accounts of the fighting that occurred within yards of the Widow Thompson's House (now the Lee's Headquarters Museum) comes from Augustus Buell who claimed to be a member of Battery B, 4th U. S. Artillery.[2] He noted that the battery formed in a small field just to the west of Mrs.

The Widow Thompson House at Larson's Motel.
"General Lee's Headquarters."

Thompson's dooryard. The battery had been split—three guns were across the railroad cut just to the north of Mrs. Thompson's stone house and three were on the south side just west of her dooryard. The half battery near Thompson's was ordered to swing 90 degrees to its left and form facing south along the Chambersburg Road to fire across the front of the advancing Confederates. This, of course, also exposed their right flank to enemy fire. As the Confederates began to advance, according to Buell,

> ...for seven or eight minutes ensued probably the most desperate fighting ever waged between artillery and infantry at close range without a particle of cover on either side. They gave us volley after volley in front and flank, and we gave them double canister as fast as we could load...Up and down the line men reeling and falling; splinters flying from wheels and axles where bullets hit; in rear, horses tearing and plunging, mad with wounds or terror; drivers yelling, shells bursting, shot shrieking overhead, howling about our ears or throwing up great clouds of dust where they struck; the musketry crashing on three sides of us; bullets hissing, humming and whistling everywhere; cannon roaring; all crash on crash and peal on peal, smoke, dust splinters, blood, wreck and carnage indescribable; but the brass guns of old B still bellowed and not a man or boy flinched or faltered! Every man's shirt soaked with sweat and many of them sopped with blood from wounds not severe enough to make such bulldogs "let go"—bareheaded, sleeves rolled up, faces blackened....[3]

The very spot occupied by the left half of Battery B, 4th U. S. Artillery is now occupied by the westernmost buildings of Larson's Motel.

Long known in the Gettysburg area as one of the finer, more intimate motels situated right on the battlefield with a perfect view of the first day's field, it rests on the site where a campground and cottages once stood. In response to the "vacation boom" which began in the 1950s, the campground was turned into Larson's Cottage Court and eventually into Larson's Motel. The current owners continue to upgrade the facility, currently constructing some luxurious suites and renovating rooms. Perhaps it is because of the changing of the physical status quo of the historic area that some unexplainable events have occurred in the vicinity.

One couple was staying in the westernmost wing of the motel. At night, that section of Gettysburg is relatively quiet. It was right around the anniversary of the battle. (Once again we must question, is it because there are so many more people to witness any random paranormal activity during the anniversary of the battle, or are the remnants of the men who fought here truly more active then, at the anniversary of their own trauma?) The man and his wife were sound asleep. Suddenly there was an explosion that rattled the walls and the mirrors in the room. The noise awakened his wife. He scrambled out of bed, grabbed his robe and sprinted outside to see what had been demolished by the explosion.

To his confusion, there was absolutely nothing outside that could have caused the loud "boom" he and his wife had heard in his room just seconds before. Not only that, there was no one else outside the building investigating the sound. That left him to conclude that he and his wife must have been the only ones to have heard it, and that the noise had been confined to their room alone. As he stood outside and his eyes became adjusted to the darkness, he realized that just before him stood two cannons and a historical marker that the government had placed there over fifty years before, marking the site where Battery B, 4th U. S. Artillery once stood.

The tear in the fabric of time—a "rip" if you will—has been referenced as the cause for visual apparitions that suddenly appear in a house, or some forlorn field, to torment the senses and sensibilities of an innocent observer. Time, like a curtain, slowly closes upon life; but it is a fragile curtain that sometimes parts then heals itself just as quickly. And who is to say that the sounds from a traumatic past event might not be able to sneak through the rip and into another time—ours. It has been recorded that voices and bugles and orders being shouted have been heard out on the darkened fields of battle. Why not regimental volleys or cannon blasts that sent men to their Maker wholesale?

Though Robert E. Lee's official headquarters tents were erected in an orchard just to the south of the Chambersburg Pike, primary sources indicate that he used the Thompson House at least part of the time. Psychic Karyol Kirkpatrick may have been shown even more information from her own "primary sources."

On Halloween morning in 1997, Karyol visited Gettysburg to participate in the local radio station's broadcast from local historic houses. She stayed in the suites across Route 30 from the Thompson House. During the broadcast she mentioned that she had gone outside the night before the broadcast and kept getting a severe pain in the right side of her neck and the left-back of her head when she stood at one corner of the house. "So there is a spirit out there that has experienced it," she said. It happened again early that morning when she visited the same corner of the house. Of course, I mentioned to her that she had described perfectly the wound suffered by Major General John F. Reynolds just a few hundred yards from where Karyol stood at the edge of the house and within her eyeshot. Mysteriously—and honestly—she said no, it was not Reynold's death that she was feeling, but someone else's. She also related how she had gone to bed the night before and awakened at about 12:30 a.m. to see a female standing over her. Karyol screamed. She later described the woman as about 5'6", wearing something pink, with some sort of wrapping on her head or perhaps a nightcap. Karyol got the distinct impression that she might be sleeping in the woman's bed. From somewhere she got the name "Miller."

Later that night, from around the closet door in that room, she saw the glow of what she called ectoplasm. She explained her definition of ectoplasm as energy that a spirit draws from humans to create a light form.

She said she felt an energy field between the two houses in the small front yard, calling it "an encampment of spirit energy." Peter Monahan, the owner of Larson's confirmed that there was a graveyard there at one time. He has a tombstone from the old cemetery. The name on it, he believed, was Reverend Miller.

Somewhere outside the building Karyol felt that there was "a trough next to a treeline" that she saw as an open mass grave. She felt an insanity and that someone wanted to commit suicide.[4]

But perhaps the most amazing things she was shown occurred in the Thompson House, the place where Lee was thought to have spent only a small amount of time. It must be remembered that Gettysburg was a huge battle and has historical details that, in some cases, are obscure to the average visitor. If you ever meet someone who claims to know everything about the battle, avoid them. The true historians of this battle will admit that they are still learning about the battle. Karyol is an infrequent visitor to this battlefield. Her knowledge of the great battle is not only limited, but she is not interested in studying it. She is often surprised when, after one of her sessions, I tell her about events at that site that are documented and that coincide with what she is "shown."

We went inside the Thompson House and toured the facility with Karyol sometimes moving a little ahead of the rest of the group. (Too many people, she has said, can sometimes be psychically distracting.) She entered the Thompson House kitchen area. The following quotes come verbatim from the tape she made for me.

She asked if "four major generals sat here and developed the tactics for communications at Devil's Den and the procedures for the next two days." Not wanting to give her any historical material before she gave us her input, no one answered. She continued with her eyes closed. She felt as though there was "a lot of confusion...it seems as though one of the generals was not happy with what was going to take place; and that he did not agree with it or was not in tune to what possibly Lee was going to do. And there was some conflict." She continued: "I felt as though Lee went out leaving the other three men to confer. But I felt as though two of the men really didn't want to take sides. There were two major men in here at a mental conflict....But there were four major generals."

She obviously meant "major" in the sense that they were important, rather than their rank being "major-general." Someone on the tape can be heard confirming that Longstreet was definitely against Lee's plans. Karyol asked, "Who were the other two?" meaning the other generals at the meeting. Since no historian who was there that morning could document Lee holding a council of war at the Thompson House, no one could be certain who else was there. It is documented, however, that Lee, James Longstreet, A. P. Hill and John Bell Hood—all "major" generals with the Army of Northern Virginia—had met near the Seminary and spread some maps out on a fallen tree and there had the controversial discussion on the proper direction of attack upon the south end of the Union line—the fight that would include the battle around Devil's Den. It is also well known in historian's circles that Longstreet argued with Lee as far as the tactics for the upcoming battle were concerned. He argued at least five times and nearly to the point of insubordination. Lee did eventually leave the conference upset.

Karyol mentioned that two of the generals refused to take sides. She identified the fact that Lee and Longstreet had a conflict. This she may have picked up from some of the background discussion in the room. But she could not have picked up what she said next, because nowhere on the tape is it mentioned: "The one general did not want to be aggressive in the battle and Lee did. And there was a conflict; Lee got mad and left. But there were four of them conferring at a table over the maps and it seems as though the tall man which I'm going to call Longstreet did not like the position or the activity to which the soldiers were going to be put in; he had scoped out the area seeing and knowing that it was going to be a most difficult attack to under go. And he had had...I hope this is documented...he had had dreams or visions or talked about that he did not see the aggression from next to the creek going up into Devil's Den working. He felt as though there was not enough artillery or whatever was needed or necessary to take that field."

Longstreet at Gettysburg, as some historians will say, was putting forth his view on warfare—an essentially modern opinion that emphasized maneuver as opposed to frontal assault. He argued this point to Lee several times during the course of the battle, then finally gave up. Lee ignored his most trusted subordinate's ideas here at Gettysburg. The results were the costly assaults through the Peach Orchard, The Wheatfield, and Devil's Den until his troops were finally stopped at Little Round Top. The climax of Lee's immovable, aggressive policy came the next day during Pickett's Charge. Pickett's Division was a part of Longstreet's Corps and so, the supreme irony: The man who was so against frontal assault at Gettysburg was forced to use his own men in carrying out just the orders he had argued against so emotionally.

Manfully, after Pickett's Charge was repulsed, Robert E. Lee admitted that, "This has been all my fault."

The ramifications of this controversy—Lee versus Longstreet; aggressive attack versus skillful, swift maneuver—can be nothing less that the difference between defeat or the distinct possibility of victory here at Gettysburg. And with Gettysburg considered by many historians to be the watershed battle of the American Civil War, and the Civil War to have been the watershed war of our nation's history, then perhaps it is no wonder that the spirit echoes of great men's emotional turmoils are imbedded deep within the walls of the Widow Thompson's house.

THE LAST COURT OF APPEAL

...After breakfast I was called by the messenger with whom I had rode the day before and who was on his return. He told me that the Confederates had withdrawn during the night. With this knowledge, I immediately mounted my horse and rode back to the town.... The wounded had been removed but the dead lay unburied and the ground was strewn with abandoned muskets, knapsacks, canteens and other accouterments of war. The houses were marked with shot and shell on both sides of the street. Some with ugly gaps in the wall and others with a well defined hole where the cannon ball had entered. A frame building particularly attracted my attention. It stood in a position facing the Union front and the weather boarding from the top to within a few feet of the ground was literally honey-combed with the Minie balls. No boards were torn or displaced but thousands of neat round holes marked the places where the balls entered.

—Leonard Marsden Gardner, *Sunset Memories*

While the National Park Service offers a seventeen mile driving tour of the part of the battlefield owned by the American public, much of the battlefield can be covered on foot—and probably should be done that way, since that is the way the soldiers themselves saw it. Not only should you get out of your car at Devil's Den and Little Round Top, but you should walk the streets of the town of Gettysburg, just as the soldiers did during those three tumultuous days in July 1863.

The town itself is not all that big. Nearly anyone can walk it in a couple of hours. And a walk through the town is a trip into the past, with the help of the several walking tours available and the assistance of a good imagination.

One can see the three Jennie Wade Houses, all still standing and marked with plaques indicating their importance in the life of the only civilian killed in the three day fight. Her birthplace—a small wooden house at 246 Baltimore Street—stands restored by a caring local businessman. The home where she lived at the time of her untimely death is just a block down Breckenridge Street from where it intersects Baltimore Street. And, of course, there is the McClellan House, where Jennie was brought down by the lead minie ball in the back and carried to the damp cellar.

There are other historic places within walking distance as well. The Dobbin House, the oldest still standing in Gettysburg, is one of the finer restaurants in the town; the Wills House where Abraham Lincoln stayed the night before he delivered the Gettysburg Address—where he actually finished the two minute speech—is now a museum. There is a cannon on the campus of Gettysburg College at the corner of Carlisle Street and Lincoln Avenue marking where Company K, First Ohio Light Artillery stopped and made a stand during the Union retreat on July 1. The open view out the Carlisle Road from this rise is self-evident as to why it was a good rear-guard position for artillery. The Gettysburg College campus holds two buildings from the battle-era, and the former burial sites outside of them that held the bodies—and the amputated limbs—of the wounded who died within the college structures.

On foot you can reach out and touch the bricks of the homes in Gettysburg marked with bronze plaques that indicate they were here at the time of the battle—you may be placing your hand where a soldier rested his weapon to fire at his fellow American. Or you may lean against an exterior wall made of that peculiar salmon-colored brick where some gentle mother's son slumped, bleeding from a horrible wound that was not there just a second before that very likely might end the life his mother gave him. Surely you will brush against an ancient sycamore tree that once felt the caress of crinoline as Gettysburg womanhood poured out its heart through hard-working hands, rushing to and fro along these very streets to care for the torn boys, remembering, perhaps, their own sons in jeopardy in some far-off town.

Pause if you will at the old Adams County Court House, built on the southwest corner of Baltimore and Middle Streets between 1858 and 1859, and moved from its prominent spot in the center square of this seat of Adams County. It was past this large brick building that Union soldiers ran on the afternoon of July 1, pursued by Confederate soldiers just a block away. Later, the courthouse, along with all the rest of the town, became the rear of the Confederate battle line. While the battle raged, the courthouse became, as did most of the buildings in and around the town, a makeshift field hospital. From Greg Coco's work on the hospitals at Gettysburg comes this observation from a woman who lived across the street:

> The sights and sounds at the courthouse for a week after the battle are too horrible to describe. Limbs were amputated amid the cries and groans of suffering humanity and often have I stopped my ears that I might not hear.... Loads of arms and legs of these poor soldiers, that were amputated...were carted outside of town, and either burned or buried....[1]

In Coco's work he quotes a wounded Confederate who entered the courthouse and saw that all the seats had been thrown out the windows. The room was lined with wounded soldiers and a row of tables in the center held a moving, writhing column of patients, squirming under the sear of the surgeons' saws and knives. Coco also relates accounts of bullets striking the brick walls and a shell exploding in the cupola of the courthouse.

Historic Adams County Court House.

Another soldier of the modern era occupied the building. It was at this courthouse that presidential candidate, Adams County resident and general Dwight D. Eisenhower registered to vote.

It is also there in our county courthouse where the records of our existence are kept: the birth records, the real estate records, marriages and divorces, lawsuits and criminal records, and finally death and estate papers; recapitulations kept, perhaps, if only for our obsession with keeping them, of the simple yet complicated truths and falsehoods, the understated tragedies, the lusts and yearnings, hopes and misfortunes and injustices, the dreams and the grief, and final statements about our very short time here in this world. In between the lines of the records can be found the most fascinating part of the human character—no, not truth, not in these records, never the real truth as we would like to believe that our records keep—but something else instead. For it is only when people try to explain why they did something, try to rationalize their actions, lie or half-lie or make excuses, that they reveal the frailty all mankind has in common, the one verity we all share.

After the Civil War the courthouse was the site of numerous postwar celebrations and speeches as the veterans returned time and again to the battle-town where they left so much of themselves, physically, emotionally, and spiritually. On the evening of October 3, 1889, in the courthouse—probably in the old courtroom, since it is the largest room in the building—Maj. Gen. Joshua Chamberlain, in dedicating the Maine monuments at Gettysburg, gave one of his most inspiring speeches. Before a large crowd, he recalled his native state's role in the tremendous struggle:

> Part and parcel of this political being of the people is the State of ours. As such she stood on these hills and slopes a generation ago, of the foremost of the people's defenders. Whether on the first, the second, or the third day's battle: whether on the right, caught and cut to pieces by the great shears-blades of two suddenly enclosing hostile columns; on the left, rolled back by a cyclone of unappeasable assault; or on the center, dashed upon in an agony of desperation, terrible, sublime; wherever there was a front, the guns of Maine thundered and her colors stood....[2]

He went on, speaking of the men he knew and commanded, and of those he knew not, but that they were from his own beloved Pine Tree State:

> Now you have gathered these bodies here. You mark their names with headstones, and compass them about with the cordon of the State's proud sorrow. You station them here, on the ground they held. Here they will remain, not buried but transfigured forms,—part of the earth they glorified,—part also of the glory that is to be....[3]

So the souls that passed along the corridors and through the doorways of the courthouse in Gettysburg are many and varied, from major generals and former presidents to the most wretched outcasts of our small society: the criminals, larcenists, and murderers.

But there are other things between the walls of the old courthouse in Gettysburg. Things that remain because of or beyond their own will. Things that remain and roam and are sometimes seen by unsuspecting individuals, caught by circumstance or necessity, in the wrong place at just the wrong time.

The courthouse is used twenty-four hours a day, for there is no timeclock that the miscreants punch: felony is a round-the-clock occupation. So often you will find law enforcement officers working after their patrol shift is finished in the old courthouse.

One such officer had been in the courthouse at night before, sometimes with another officer, sometimes alone, and had seen—according to his estimate—some 10 or 12 times, a strange, hazy mist about the size of a man levitate slowly across the courthouse lobby from one side to the other. Can you imagine being alone in that building and in that lobby where walked the doomed murderers from the police vehicles to the courtroom, and looking up unsuspectingly to see the scene reenacted time and time again by the shadows of the doomed? And to see the spectral light more than once, and to never know when you will see it again. It indeed takes a special person to be a police officer.

And this particular night, in the basement of the building, where everyone from future presidents to Civil War era surgeons once stalked that corridor, the policeman sat with his back to the door to the hallway. Across from him was another officer. All the doors to the courthouse were locked—every policeman knows to lock all the doors when in the building to assure that no one can come in and surprise you. The only danger is that you might be locking someone else in. They were both silent, engaged in doing paperwork. The second officer was aware of what the other had, at times, seen in the courthouse. He was interested, but not alarmed or impressed. That would change momentarily.

It was approaching 3:00 a.m., the time their shift was about to expire. Everything in the old courthouse was quiet, except for those few odd noises a very old building is prone to. Something caught the second officer's eye. He looked up from his work just in time to catch the shadow of a man passing slowly across the doorway. A quizzical look crossed his face. The other officer with his back to the door asked what was the problem. Alerted to a potential danger, he stood and walked to the door and looked into the hallway. There, in the hall was what he described as a "grayish, human-sized, floating figure," passing down the corridor. By the time the second officer reached the door, the figure had disappeared down the hallway.

Both officers followed the path of the intruder, but by then, there was no sign of him. Further investigation was futile. Somewhere in the edifice that has housed everything from presidents and generals, to criminals of the worst kind, to the helpless wounded and the corpses of the glorious dead, he had simply vanished.

Historic Adams County Court House lobby.

ENDNOTES

A Special Hell

1. Garry L. Adelman and Timothy H. Smith, *Devil's Den: A History and Guide* (Gettysburg, PA: Thomas Publications, 1997).
2. There has been some controversy over exactly where Smith's guns were located. Some historians place them higher on the hill. At the wall they would have had cover in front of the gunners and would have occupied the "military crest" of the hill, which is not the top but just below the top of any hill so that they would not be silhouetted against the sky, thus making good targets.
3. Adelman and Smith, 42.
4. Ibid., 45.
5. These and other fascinating stories can be found in Garry Adelman's and Timothy H. Smith's comprehensive book, *Devil's Den: A History and Guide.* It is highly recommended as the complete history of the area known as Devil's Den.
6. See Mark Nesbitt, *Ghosts of Gettysburg* (Gettysburg, PA: Thomas Publications, 1991),17-20 for more recent stories of Devil's Den and the Triangular Field.
7. Every psychic I have worked with has an absolutely negative reaction when I even mention the name of the board game that many take as a child's toy. I have seen them physically turn away from me when I mention it or take a quick step back. The Ouija Board, they say almost universally, can be a direct gateway into the other world—and not the other world of light, but of darkness and deception. It is definitely not a plaything, according to them.
8. See Mark Nesbitt, *Ghosts of Gettysburg III* (Gettysburg, PA: Thomas Publications, 1995), 21-28 for the accounts of paranormal happenings at the encampment for the motion picture *Gettysburg.*

Blood on the Moon

1. In the ensuing years and jumble of my writing life, I have retained the photo, but lost the names of the individuals who sent it to me. I do remember speaking with one, however, and, at this point, I wish to thank them for their fascinating, yet unexplainable photo.
2. In his letter, the photographer wrote that he submitted the photo for me to try to explain to him what it might be, but he also admitted that he would like to

believe that it was a ghost from the three terrible days in July 1863. He also admitted that his camera upon occasion will produce a light glare under similar conditions. He did not say that he believes this to be a light glare and it does not fit the definition of a lens flare. My interest in it stems from its incredible similarity to the other photo.

Sleepers, Awake!

1. *The War of the Rebellion: A Compilation of the Official Records of the Union and Confederate Armies*, Series I, Vol. XXVII, Pt. 2, (Washington, D.C.: U.S. Government Printing Office, 1880-1901), 649-50. Hereafter cited as *O.R.*

2. Gregory A. Coco, *Wasted Valor: The Confederate Dead at Gettysburg* (Gettysburg, PA: Thomas Publications, 1990), 63.

The Quick and the Dead

1. Mark Nesbitt, *More Ghosts of Gettysburg* (Gettysburg, PA: Thomas Publications, 1992), 85-86.

Fate's Children

1. *O.R.*, Series I, Vol. XXVII, Pt. 2, Report of Col. John T. Mercer, 21st Georgia Infantry states, "the Twenty-first Georgia was ordered to hold the street leading from the court-house to the eastward."

The Bridge to Nowhere

1. Colonel Jacob M. Sheads related this story to me nearly thirty years ago. It was one of the first ghost stories I collected.

2. Kathy Georg Harrison, from an unpublished paper and documentation in the files of the Gettysburg National Military Park archives.

3. Chamberlain at the Dedication of Maine Monuments at Gettysburg, October 3, 1889. From Joshua Lawrence Chamberlain, *"Bayonet! Forward": My Civil War Reminiscences* (Gettysburg, PA: Stan Clark Military Books, 1994). Stan Clark collected Chamberlain's most famous speeches and writings in this fine book. I highly recommend it to any Chamberlain buff.

Death's High Holiday

1. Edwin B. Coddington, *The Gettysburg Campaign: A Study in Command* (New York: Charles Scribner's Sons, 1968), 357.

2. Glenn Tucker, *High Tide at Gettysburg* (Dayton, OH: Press of Morningside Bookshop, 1973), 205-208.

3. Nesbitt, *Ghosts of Gettysburg*, 13; *More Ghosts of Gettysburg*, 45.

Field of Sorrows

1. Coco, *A Vast Sea of Misery*, 20-21.

2. Nesbitt, *Ghosts of Gettysburg III*, 46-48.
3. Actually, I have no reason to "test" Karyol. I believe she has an incredible gift and has finely tuned her senses over the years so that she is remarkably receptive to whatever subtle signals the residuals of history leave upon their surroundings. I set up the "test" for others, so that no one can say I coached her.

The First Deaths
1. For a detailed analysis of Henry Heth's justification for bringing on the battle, see Mark Nesbitt, *Saber and Scapegoat* (Mechanicsburg, PA: Stackpole Books, 1994), 85-86; 134-139.
2. Although Buell wrote a number of articles (which eventually became a book) in which he claimed to be a member of Battery B, the National Archives has no record of him being in the outfit. If Buell never served with the battery, he must have interviewed a number of the surviving members; nearly all agreed, including the commander of the battery, that Buell's articles were both factual and accurate.
3. Augustus Buell, *The Cannoneer: Story of a Private Soldier* (Washington, D.C.: National Tribune, 1890) 67-70.
4. See Mark Nesbitt's story "The Premature Burial" in *Ghosts of Gettysburg III* for details of events at this site.

The Last Court of Appeal
1. Coco, *A Vast Sea of Misery*, 22.
2. Chamberlain, *Bayonet! Forward: My Civil War Reminiscences*, 201.
3. Ibid.

Such were the remnants of that great company of heroic souls named the Army of the Potomac. Knowing full well the meaning of such words as hardship and suffering, facing unknown fields of sorrows yet to come, they stood fast by their consecration, offering all there is in manhood for the sake of what is best in man.

—Major General Joshua L. Chamberlain

Mark Nesbitt was born in Lorain, Ohio. He graduated from Baldwin-Wallace College, Berea, Ohio, with a BA in English literature. He worked for the National Park Service as a ranger historian for 5 years and started his own freelance writing and research business in 1977.

Other books by Mark Nesbitt:

Ghosts of Gettysburg

More Ghosts of Gettysburg

Ghosts of Gettysburg III

If the South Won Gettysburg

35 Days to Gettysburg: The Campaign Diaries of Two American Enemies

Rebel Rivers: A Guide to Civil War Sites on the Potomac, Rappahannock, York, and James

Saber and Scapegoat: J.E.B. Stuart and the Gettysburg Controversy

Through Blood and Fire: The Selected Civil War Papers of Maj. Gen. Joshua Chamberlain

Drummer Boy at Gettysburg

Flickertail's Friends.

THOMAS PUBLICATIONS publishes books about the American Colonial era, the Revolutionary War, the Civil War, and other important topics. For a complete list of titles, please visit our web site at:

http://civilwarreader.com/thomas

Or write to:

THOMAS PUBLICATIONS
P.O. Box 3031
Gettysburg, PA 17325